Honor:
The Law That
Governs
Greatness

Jamelle D. Sanders

DEDICATION

This book is dedicated to my incredible parents Jeff & Michelle Sanders. Everything that I am today is because of your love, support, and belief in me. You gave me much more than love and an amazing family. You gave me a spiritual foundation that has anchored me and empowered me to live a life of unlimited possibilities and opportunities. I can never repay you for everything that you have given to me. However, I will spend the rest of my life honoring the sacrifices that you made for me.

CONTENTS

INTRODUCTION

"Dishonor is the seed for the
disintegrating of
the significance of the human soul."
-Jamelle Sanders

Well, after I write a book I always take a break. I feel like it is important to rest and reset after the long process of writing a book. Honestly, I am often so tired that I cannot even think about what the next project will be. However, this time it was really different for me. I was ready to jump back into the writing process. I knew that the follow up to *Significance* was going to be critical. I have so many ideas in my head but I believe in being on the cutting-edge. I always endeavor to put my finger on the prophetic pulse of culture and bring a message of empowerment that will shift and transform lives. I believe that we are at a critical moment in history. We have officially crossed over into the next decade. As a visionary leader, I can tell you that this decade will be nothing like the last decade. We are on the precipice of major breakthroughs, discoveries, and innovations. Industries will be radically transformed and shifted in the next ten years. This is a critical moment and I want you to be

Introduction

prepared for the shift. I do not want you to get left behind. It is one of the reasons that I felt that I needed to write this book now. I could not afford to put this off for a later time. The information that I am about to share with you will empower you to navigate this season of uncertainty and change in the world. The insights in this book will be critical to your calling and empower you to maintain your edge in an ever-changing and ever-evolving world.

While many of you are familiar with my writing and my writing style, I know that some of you are being introduced to me for the very first time. This book will not be like anything you have read before. I am not interested in just putting out content that does not add value and enrich the lives of people around the world. I have committed myself to a life of excellence and I have set new standards in the self-empowerment space. In fact, over a decade ago when I started using the term self-empowerment nobody knew what I was talking about. I write to speak to the context of culture and to be a prophetic catalyst of change. I write to empower you to do the inner work that will propel you into a life of focus, freedom, and fulfillment. I hope that this book will not just inspire and motivate you. My prayer is that this book will shake you to your core and empower you to shift the course of your life. If you truly grasp this principle, your life will not just grow but flourish. This complex principle will empower you to build capacity, bring solutions to industry and shape culture in a profound way. Get ready to go on an adventure!

Introduction

"You cannot demand honor without first living an honorable life."
-Jamelle Sanders

Honor is so much more than a book. This is a prophetic message to generations that will come after me. One of the reasons I write so much is because I am creating a mindshare that I can leave on the earth for generations to come. Long after I am gone, my thoughts and ideas will continue to empower and uplift generations to come. I believe that the principles outlined in this book will radically transform your life. Many people look at my life today and they marvel at my success. While I could share many things that contributed to my success today, I believe that my understanding of the law of honor was the seed that unlocked unlimited greatness in my life. As many of you know, I am respected around the world as a thought leader. How did I get here? How have I grown my influence? How have I stayed consistent? Why do so many people admire me and the work that I am doing around the world? I am going to answer some of these questions in the pages of this book. I hope that you will not just glance at the pages of this book. It is my sincere desire that you will grow through every page of this book. Also, I hope that you will do the exercises that follow each chapter. Do the inner work and empower yourself to become a leader of honor and influence in the world. You were born for so much more than an ordinary life. As a global influencer, I want to challenge you today to pursue excellence and create an extraordinary life.

As you can see, I am loaded and ready to share wisdom and insights with you that will change your life forever. *Honor* is a law and a principle that changed the trajectory of my life. This principle has empowered my progression, promotion, and prosperity. This is not just an idea that I believe in. The principle of honor is a life constitution for me. In other words, this is a paradigm and a way of life for me. The principle of honor shapes my mindset, my relationships, my brand, my faith and every single thing that I do. This principle took me from the back and moved me to the front. When I learned the power of honor, it unlocked doors, changed my relationship constellation, unleashed my true capacity, and gave me the courage to conquer new frontiers. In fact, I had gifts, talents, and abilities in me that I did not even have a clue that I possessed. However, when I learned the law of honor I tapped into latent talents and abilities. I am doing things today that I never imagined I could do. I attribute it all to the law of honor. Honor is a law that regulates the universe and not enough people are aware of it. It is not that the law has been hidden. What I have discovered is that the laws and principles that govern success are often coveted but not communicated. I made a vowel that when I succeeded I would reach back and share the wisdom and insights that shaped my success. Many people want greatness but they will never manifest greatness without honor. You will never mount certain platforms without honor. You cannot fulfill purpose and maximize your greatest potential without honor. *Honor* is a principle that will revolutionize individuals, organizations, governments, and generations. Get ready because I am about to give you a key that will unlock your prophetic destiny!

Part 1: Potential

"Potential is a seed that must be cultivated
in order to flourish."
-Jamelle Sanders

CHAPTER 1: HIDDEN IN OBSCURITY

"All great leaders are hidden in obscurity until
their moment of revealing comes."
-Jamelle Sanders

19 So Elijah went and found Elisha son of Shaphat
plowing a field. There were twelve teams of oxen in
the field, and Elisha was plowing with the twelfth
team. Elijah went over to him and threw his cloak
across his shoulders and then walked away. 20 Elisha
left the oxen standing there, ran after Elijah, and said
to him, "First let me go and kiss my father and mother
good-bye, and then I will go with you!"
Elijah replied, "Go on back, but think about what I
have done to you."
21 So Elisha returned to his oxen and slaughtered
them. He used the wood from the plow to build a fire
to roast their flesh. He passed around the meat to the
townspeople, and they all ate. Then he went with
Elijah as his assistant. -1st Kings 19:19-21

In this text, we find Elisha in the field
plowing. He was unknown and in the middle of a
prophetic process. Many of you reading this book can
relate to Elisha. You feel like you are all alone in a
field trying to cultivate the gifts that God has given
you. Deep down inside you know that you have been
destined for greatness. However, you have confused

the field of development with the field of destiny. What you have to understand is that where you are right now is not your place of destiny. Elisha had a global prophetic ministry locked up in him. Yet we find him here in the field plowing with twelve yoke of oxen. It does not sound like the backdrop for a story of greatness. However, these few verses are pregnant with prophetic insights that have the power to shift and revolutionize your life. I have been where many of you are and I know exactly what you are going through. You are uncomfortable because you are right in the middle of prophetic development and prophetic process. You feel uneasy and unsettled. You are desperate for this season of your life to come to an end. You want to manifest greatness and do great things in your lifetime and generation. However, you do not understand the law of time and the law of process.

The law of time states that God synchronizes and syncopates our lives according to His rhythm and timing. In fact, Psalm 31:15 states "My times are in thy hand: deliver me from the hand of mine enemies, and from them that persecute me." In other words, there is a divine timing and sequencing to your life. From more than twenty years of experience, I can tell you that you never want to be behind time and you never want to get ahead of time. When you are behind time, then you are missing out on divine moments of opportunity to grow, develop and stretch your capacity. On the other hand, to be ahead of time means that you are moving faster than God. It means that you are out of the timing of God. More importantly, you are not in sync with the plan and the purpose of God for your life. Process is essential because it resets us and repositions us in the center of God's will for our lives. Discomfort is God's way of divinely positioning you with His will and His purpose for your life. We all have plans for our lives but it is God's plan for your life that will prevail. You can be persistent about getting your own way. However, you paralyze your life and punish your potential when you fail to align with God's will for your life. You have to understand that you were created in eternity and birthed into time. While it can be easy to think that you are in control, you must understand that God sits outside of time and yet dictates what happens within the confines of time. So your life is not your own. You are on a prophetic timetable and there is a specific purpose and assignment that you are to fulfill in your lifetime and generation. The ultimate objective of time is to serve your purpose. When time is not serving your purpose, you are wasting moments and squandering opportunities.

The other thing we do not understand is the law of process. The law of process states that the legal growth, maturation and development of your life cannot occur without process. In other words, anything that you are not processed to is illegal in your life. What we have is a generation of people that are gifted but they refuse to grow. We have a generation that wants to mount platforms that they have not been processed to stand on. Everybody wants destiny but nobody wants to be developed. Anything that lacks development is disposable and not built to last. The process of a thing is what determines the price of a thing. I do not know about you but I am not a fan of cheap products. I am willing to pay extra to ensure that I am buying a product that is built to last. Well, if you want to be a sustainable leader then you must be willing to develop. Ecclesiates 3:11 states "He has made every thing beautiful in its time: also he has put eternity in men's hearts, so that no man can find out the work that God does from the beginning to the end." In other words, you have to be willing to cooperate with the process and trust the timing of your life. So many people have developed a negative perspective about time. However, as someone that has trained and empowered leaders around the world I know the value of time. When you are young you think that you have all the time in the world. However, as you mature you realize that time is a gift that God uses to engineer your growth. More importantly, time is the seed for the development of your potential. Time is the prophetic tool that God uses to bring you into your prophetic process. We all have a dream and a vision that God has placed in our hearts concerning our futures. How do we realize those dreams? We realize those dreams by allowing God to take us through a prophetic process. We realize our dreams by making the most of every moment of the process and letting God mold us so we can maximize our greatest potential. Never despise development in your life. Your value is not defined by the platforms that you mount. Your value is defined by the process that promotes you onto great platforms in life. Development is not only a catalyst to success. Development is the only thing that gives credibility to your success. Self promotion may get you on the stage temporarily. However, when you submit to process you produce something that is timeless and invaluable.

Elisha was in the middle of a prophetic process. I am sure at the time that it seemed trivial and unimportant. After all, he was simply working in the family business and simply plowing with the twelve yoke of oxen. Elisha had no clue that the field was simply developing him for his prophetic destiny. Elisha had no clue that in the mundane tasks of everyday life God was molding a prophetic voice that would one day change the world. The problem with the world today is that everybody wants to be big and everybody despises a small beginning. However, I am grateful for my small beginning. I am grateful for the years that I worked hard in silence and nobody knew who I was. I can still remember the years where I was simply taking out the garbage, cleaning bathrooms, helping behind the scenes and just happy to serve in any way that I could. I was not trying to be recognized or to look important. I just had a heart to serve and I was willing to help to the best of my ability. I would not trade anything for my field because it forged in me character, commitment, consistency and capacity. I would not be who I am today without the field. Elisha had no clue that one day God would bring him before kings and world leaders. He had no idea that God would work miracles, signs and wonders through the same hands that were plowing in the field. We have too many people that are ready to abandon the field of development. However, if you abandon the field of development you will abort the field of destiny. Do not forfeit your prophetic future simply because you do not like the field.

It was in the field that I developed a relationship with God. Some people are offended and insulted when I talk about my Chrisitan faith. However, I always say that spirituality is the foundation of all my success. Without spirituality my life is absolutely nothing. The field is a place of prophetic gold. The field is the place where valuable gems are hidden and only discerning eyes have the perception to see the value in a field. Many people will read about the early years of Elisha and call his life boring. However, they do not realize that it is in the field that God forms you and forges greatness within you. You are so ready to fulfill your destiny but you have not been forged for destiny. In other words, there is an inner work that has to take place in you before you can ever have influence in the world. It is dangerous to give power to a person that has not been processed. Power without process produces parasitic leadership. Power without process makes one prideful and egotistical. On the other hand, power coupled with process produces preservational leadership. In other words, when you are developed you not only succeed but you sustain your success. Many of you reading this book are in the field right now. God has hidden you in obscurity for a season. You have to stop seeing obscurity as a curse. You must learn to view obscurity as an opportunity to prepare for greatness in your life. God uses obscurity to order your steps into prophetic destiny. What I have learned over the last twenty plus years is that you do not want to be revealed before you are ready. God will never expose you to the world without first expanding and evolving you. You cannot rush your release date. You cannot manipulate your moment. Obscurity is necessary so that you do not allow the field to define you when it is only for your development. Many times when we encounter obscurity we think that God has forgotten us. On the contrary, God has not forgotten you but He is forging Himself within you. The field is often a dark and lonely place. However, the greatest development always happens in dark places. Refuse to be bitter about your field. Resolve within yourself that you are going to allow your field to build you for prophetic destiny.

When you curse your field you ultimately curse your future. Elisha could have complained or become bitter about his field. However, Elisha did not complain about his field because he understood that it was a catalyst to prophetic destiny. Elisha understood that if he remained faithful to his field then one day God would fulfill his dream and usher him into prophetic destiny. Elisha had a revelation that if you are willing to sow into your field with expectation that it becomes a place of supernatural encounters. Many of us are sowing into our fields with frustration and as a result we are creating cycles of failure and defeat in our lives. You cannot curse where God has planted you and expect to prosper. Some of you reading this book have convinced yourself that your field is unnecessary. However, your field is a place of learning, growth, maturity, development and adjustment. It is the place where God builds you so you can become who you were born to be. Elisha understood that the field was a seed for his prophetic future. What field have you sown your life into? I see far too many people that want fields to reward them for seeds that they have never sown. They never cooperate with process yet they want to make progress and prosper. They continue to get off of the wheel because they refuse to be molded for God's mission for their lives. The field is a prophetic portrait of sacrifice. What I have discovered is that sacrifice is the womb of significance. Any person that is not willing to sow the seed of sacrifice will never qualify for a life of success.

Are you cursing your field and crippling your future? It is time for you to get yourself together. Understand that you are being hidden in obscurity so you can be developed for heaven's agenda. The field is not about your comfort. The field is about your conformity to the divine will. If you will allow the field to serve its purpose in your life, then you will change your perception and realize that everything is serving as a catalyst into your prophetic destiny. It will make sense to you why God has taken you through a season of frustration, isolation and development. It will become clear that what you thought was punishment was really God proving you. You will come to a place of awakening in your life where you realize that the field was for your protection and development. God has been using your field to get you ready for your big reveal. Your time of exposure is coming but first God has to reset you to His eternal plan for your life. The plan that God had for you before you were ever formed in your mother's womb. You will no longer say that the field is a waste of time. The field is God's way of transforming you for your Kingdom assignment. Stop running from the field. The longer you delay development the longer you delay your destiny. There are no shortcuts to success and no cliff notes for your calling. You have to be proven in order to be promoted. Your faithfulness to the field is where God plants you, processes you and prepares you to fulfill your purpose, maximize your potential and make an impact. The field is necessary in order for you to step into your prophetic future. Elisha was faithful to his field and as a result God found him in the field. Will God find you in your field? Are you willing to let your faithfulness unlock your prophetic future? The field that you are willing to sow into today is the same field that God will select you from tomorrow. Treasures are always hidden in obscurity.

Elisha was willing to work his field and be faithful. I am admonishing you to work your field. It may not be the ideal place. However, invest in the field and watch God invite you into your prophetic future. Your life may not look anything like you want it to look right now. However, if you will be faithful in the field that you are planted, I guarantee that you will flourish and prosper. We live in an era where many people expect overnight success. As I always say, I am a thirty year overnight success. In other words, what you see today has taken over three decades to unfold in my life. Guess what? I never abandoned the field no matter how frustrated I was. I had moments where I could have easily walked away from the field and pursued other interests. However, I have discovered that what you are invested in you cannot walk away from. You abandon things that are not valuable to you. When God first spoke to me about my destiny I was around the age of sixteen. It was many years before I started to see the unfolding of God's plan for my life. In the middle of my waiting, I made a vowel that God would find me working my field. I would sweep the floor, pick up trash, clean toilets, mop floors, and any other tasks that others deemed insignificant. I knew God had called me to greatness and I was not going to let anything get me out of the timing of God. The field is where God breaks you so that you can benefit the Kingdom. Many people want to be blessed but very few are willing to be broken.

Fields are where agendas die and assignments are born. It was in the field that God spoke to me as a sixteen-year-old and told me that I would one day impact the world. It was in the field that I learned the voice of God, sharpened my prophetic edge and learned how to walk by faith. Some people associate the field with shame. On the other hand, I will always see my field as a place of significance. No matter how high God takes me, when I look at my field I am overcome with humility. When you truly understand that your life is not your own, you will stop competing for positions and titles. Instead, you will start unleashing your capacity for greatness. You will realize that there is no room for ego in the eternal plan of God. So many people are clamoring for a platform when God is trying to put something in you that will bless nations and generations. God can only form Himself in you if you remain in the field. Elisha was in his field plowing and God used that field to position him for prophetic destiny. What some would consider mundane and ordinary was where Elisha was mantled to fulfill God's original plan and purpose. Elisha's place of obscurity became his place of opportunity. Obscurity is always the womb by which God births the next leaders, trailblazers, world shakers and history shapers. It is always the individuals that are in the field that seem to be forgotten that God puts on the frontlines for Kingdom advancement. You cannot be found if you are not willing to be faithful to the field. I am grateful that I was hidden in obscurity because I am now fulfilling what heaven ordered. Fields are not places of containment. Fields are places of capacity building. Obscurity is where God builds in you the capacity to fulfill your prophetic destiny. Obscurity was one of the greatest gifts in my life. Obscurity is what groomed me to manifest greatness!

.

Honorable Living Exercises

1. Can you relate to Elisha being in the field?

2. Are you using time to fulfill your purpose?

3. Are you cooperating with the process?

4. Have you cursed your field or are you cultivating your field?

5. Is your field a place of containment or capacity building?

CHAPTER 2: THE INNER PROMPTING

"More is always available but you must reach
for it."
-Jamelle Sanders

19 So Elijah went and found Elisha son of Shaphat
plowing a field. There were twelve teams of oxen in
the field, and Elisha was plowing with the twelfth
team. Elijah went over to him and threw his cloak
across his shoulders and then walked away. 20 Elisha
left the oxen standing there, ran after Elijah, and said
to him, "First let me go and kiss my father and mother
good-bye, and then I will go with you!"
Elijah replied, "Go on back, but think about what I
have done to you."
21 So Elisha returned to his oxen and slaughtered
them. He used the wood from the plow to build a fire
to roast their flesh. He passed around the meat to the
townspeople, and they all ate. Then he went with
Elijah as his assistant. 1st Kings 19:19-21

So we have established the importance of the
field. In fact, the field is such a pregnant concept that
I could write several more chapters just about the

power and purpose of the field. However, for the sake of time I will move on and discuss more important topics. Elisha was found in the field plowing with the twelve yoke of oxen. It is very interesting that Elisha was not found in a palace or a castle. Nor do we find Elisha in a key leadership role or position. We find Elisha in the field doing what some would call menial tasks. What I have discovered over the years is that the menial is often what gives birth to the meaningful in our lives. More importantly, it is how we handle the menial that determines the extent of our metron and mantle. The field could have confined Elisha if he allowed himself to be conflicted. So many times when our lives do not look like what we have dreamed of we become disappointed, disillusioned, doubtful and despondent. Yet we do not see any of these qualities being exhibited in the life of Elisha. Ecclesiastes 3:1 states that "to every thing there is a season, and a time to every purpose under the heaven." In my study over the years, I have learned that there are over thirty life cycles and each cycle holds significance and importance in our lives. It is vitally important that you never curse a cycle in your life. When you curse a cycle you cripple change and advancement in your life. How do you curse a cycle? You curse a cycle when you do not appreciate the value of a cycle in your life. Also, you curse a cycle when you do not discern the wisdom and insights that a cycle contains. Furthermore, you curse a cycle when you do not understand the purpose of a cycle in your life. You must master cycles if you want to consistently manifest change in your life.

Unfortunately, I see too many people in the world today that do not respect cycles. Therefore, they spend their entire lives on stutter repeating cycles and never realizing change in their lives. Elisha understood that he was in the middle of a prophetic process. He was devoted to his field but also discerning of the shifting of a cycle in his life. Thankfully, Elisha was prophetic and had prophetic acumen, acuity and perceptivity. This means that he was much more aware of the prophetic significance of times, seasons and moments in his life. Most people are not prophetic and they are not as perceptive to important moments and shifts in life. It is important that you do not just operate with sight but that you live your life with clear vision. Many people are in the correct field but a lack of clarity will cost them their futures. You cannot afford to allow anything to contaminate your vision or short circuit your faith. Many of you reading this book are in a season of frustration and stagnation in your life. What I have discovered is that frustration is not just an attitude. Frustration is a spirit that has an objective to make you forfeit your prophetic destiny. It was frustration that caused Moses to strike the rock when God told him to speak to it. It was frustration that caused Abraham and Sarah to try to use human ingenuity to manifest the promise of Issac. In the process, they produced an Ishmael and we are still seeing the consequences of that decision. It was frustration that caused Esau to sell his birthright to Jacob. Ultimately, it is frustration that wants to make you forfeit your prophetic destiny and abort your dreams. When you have prophetic insight and acumen you are able to see beyond today and see the beautiful possibilities of tomorrow. Frustration wants to bring you into stagnation and ultimately rob you of manifestation in your life.

How can you remain committed to the field and not allow frustration to cost you your prophetic future? The picture of your future must become bigger than the pain of your frustration. In other words, what God has promised you must become more real to you than the pressure and resistance that you are experiencing in your life. You cannot afford to allow right now to become the enemy to the realization of your dreams. Proverbs 29:18 records "where there is no vision, the people perish: but he that keepeth the law, happy is he." In other words, vision is what will carry you through the seasons of frustration in your life. Vision is a spiritual discipline that empowers you to step into your prophetic destiny. Most importantly, vision is what empowers you to fight for your future. This is why I stated that you cannot despise the field. Elisha understood that God planted him in the field to prepare him for his prophetic future. In the midst of the planting, God was purging, proving, preparing and processing him to step into his Kingdom assignment. What most people do not understand is that in those seasons of preparation is where the seed of your potential is being developed. As you grow, you are getting glimpses of the greatness that God has called you to. Without a strong vision those seasons of pressure and proving will cause the abortion of prophetic destiny. You must guard against abortion by guarding your atmosphere and governing what you give your attention to.

I just want to unpack these two concepts as briefly as I can. You must guard your atmosphere when you are pregnant with a prophetic promise. Elisha understood that he was pregnant with a global prophetic ministry that would one day influence nations. At the same time, Elisha understood that he was in a season of proving and that God had planted him in the field of development to get him ready for the field of destiny. Elisha understood that if he failed to guard the atmosphere that greatness would be aborted in his life. What do I mean by guarding the atmosphere? Elisha had to have the ability to stay focused on his future even in seasons of frustration. Elisha could not afford to allow his emotions to influence the eternal plan of God for his life. More importantly, Elisha had to constantly remind himself that the field was not permanent and that he needed to be able to perceive shifts in his life. You cannot afford to allow where you are to dictate where God has assigned you to be. Do not get comfortable in the place that God is using to build capacity in your life. Your field is not your place of residence. Your field is where God is building the resolve in you to fulfill your purpose and maximize your greatest potential. In addition, you must govern what you give your attention to. Attention is the womb of advancement, enlargement and expansion. Whatever you focus on is what will fill your life. Too many times we focus on tension, toxicity and temporary conditions in our lives. What you give your attention to will always define what you attract into your life. You cannot attract your future as long as you are giving your attention to your failures. Attention guides intention and ultimately shapes what you manifest in your life. Elisha understood that he had to give his Kingdom assignment his undivided attention. While he did not have all the pieces yet, he had prophetic acumen and acuity to stay aligned with God's prophetic timetable for his life.

When God has called you to greatness, you must be willing to contend for the unfolding of God's plan for your life. You contend by deploying the strategy of prophetic warfare. 1st Timothy 1:18 says "this charge I commit unto thee, son Timothy, according to the prophecies which went before on thee, that thou by them mightest war a good warfare." Prophetic warfare is when you rehearse the prophetic words over your life for the record books of heaven and to be heard by the ears of hell. Prophetic warfare is seeding your prophetic future with prophetic declarations and apostolic decrees. Elisha was not just plowing with twelve yoke of oxen. Elisha was seeding his future by unleashing the prophetic force of his words. Elisha was seeing into the future and seeing the day when he would come into the prophetic fulfillment of that which God had destined for his life. How was he able to see into the future? How was he able to perceive beyond the immediacy of the field into the inevitabilities of his future? Elisha was able to see beyond the mundane responsibilities of the field and into the manifestation of his prophetic future because of something that I call prophetic promptings. Elisha was plowing with twelve yoke of oxen. Twelve is a number of government and order. In other words, Elisha had a life that was in order and governed by the word of God. You will never be positioned for divine opportunities as long as you violate the law of divine order. In other words, Elisha's ability to stay in position helped to shape the prophetic possibilities of his life. Misalignment will never bring manifestation. Distractions are always sent into your life to displace you. Whatever you allow to break your focus has the authority to bankrupt your future. Can you stay postured even when you are under pressure? Can you allow the pressure in your life to provoke your prophetic future? Your ability to remain unmovable orchestrates the unfolding of God's plan for your life. Elisha also lived a life that was governed by truth. Whatever governs your life determines the growth, maturity and advancement of your life. Ultimately, what governs your life is what guides your life. Often we see time as a delayer and not a developer. As a result, we become frustrated with the lack of results and therefore we start violating spiritual laws. You cannot secure your future without a strong spiritual foundation. You cannot allow time, distractions or delays to make you abandon the anchors that authorize and credentialize your anointing and mantle. Elisha never saw time as an instrument of opposition. Instead Elisha always viewed time as an investment that would unlock opportunities in his life.

Prophetic promptings or inner promptings are supernatural moments in which you are prompted from within about shifts, turns, pivots, warnings, redirections and calibrations. Prophetic promptings also bring clarity, wisdom, insights, direction, perception and divine secrets concerning your prophetic destiny. In other words, it is when you feel a prophetic prompting or stirring that results in you taking a prophetic action. For example, when God gave me the vision for Jamelle Sanders International years ago I did not act on it immediately. In fact, God was speaking to me about the vision years before it was time for me to actually start the business. However, I remember the exact moment when God said it was time to act. It was an inner prompting and stirring and I knew that I needed to do it immediately. In addition, I was given key details, key relationships and key resources to make the vision a reality. It did not make a lot of sense to me at the time. It seemed like I was hidden in obscurity and I felt like I lacked so many resources to make the vision a reality. When I felt that inner prompting, I knew it was time to act and I was not going to allow anything to stop me. The field is an important place and so many people despise the field. Elish was plowing with those twelve yoke of oxen. Plowing is prophetic of prayer. In other words, Elisha was in a posture of prophetic intercession. As a result, Elisha was not just planted in a field but Elisha was planting the heavens. Elisha was getting downloads and uploads from heaven concerning his Kingdom assignment. If you have followed my work over the years, you know that prayer is the hallmark of my life and success. I do not commit to anything until I have first committed it to prayer. It was prayer that empowered Elisha to put his finger on the prophetic pulse of heaven. Elisha did not despise the field because it taught him how to tune out this three dimensional world and tune into the big conversation happening around the throne of God. Elisha was receiving inner promptings that would empower his inner man so that he could fulfill God's original plan and purpose for his life. The more Elisha aligned with heaven the more he was empowered to advance beyond hostile forces and satanic impositions. Elisha realized that God was using the field to attune his ears to heavens frequency and empowering him to one day become a great Kingdom force.

Are you picking up the prophetic promptings and stirrings of heaven? Many of you know exactly what I am talking about. You sense it and you feel it. While most people are not skilled at articulating these promptings and stirrings, I am here to give context to this prophetic expression. It is not instinct or gut reaction. What you are feeling is the force of pressure pointing you in the direction of your prophetic future. You cannot stay small and you know that you have been called to greatness. That inner prompting is a divine stirring within you to push the boundaries of your potential, stretch your faith, expand your capacity and enlarge your borders. The inner prompting is that part of you that knows you were made for more and that deep place in you that refuses to embrace the status quo or mediocrity. It was the same fire and force in Elisha that knew that he would not spend the rest of his life in the field. Elisha knew that a shift was coming into his life. He could perceive it and he was positioned for it. Many of you reading this book are in the middle of a prophetic process. In fact, some of you were just about ready to abandon your field but for some reason you decided to pick up this book. I am here as a prophetic voice to tell you that now is not the time to abandon the field. You have to work your field so that you do not waste your future. Many people read this text and just see Elisha working in the family business. However, they fail to see a man that lived a life of order that was totally governed by the word of God. Elisha was a prophet in the making. He did not have a platform, prestige or popularity. However, Elisha had a word over his life and he knew that God was preparing him for his collision with prophetic destiny. Elisha quietly worked his field without complaint or protest. Elisha realized that cultivating his field would one day lead him to a collision with his prophetic destiny. You cannot afford to forsake the field when it is framing your prophetic future. The very field you have labeled as a restriction in your life is the launching pad for the release of your greatest potential.

I remember when I was prompted from within. It was an uncomfortable season in my life. I had been rejected, persecuted, ridiculed and mocked. Now God was telling me to step out of my comfort zone again and to dare to pursue a dream that He put in my heart. How was I going to empower the world? Would anyone listen to me? Was I really ready? One day I stopped asking what if and I said what will be the consequences if I don't? As I took a step of faith, God reminded me of all the years I spent in the field seeding my future. Every single time I took a step God empowered me to seize my future. The vision started coming together, relationships were forged, networks were built, favor was granted, influence was given to me and God has blown my mind time and time again. The inner prompting is when we have to decide between living small and living a life of significance. You cannot stay small and the inner prompting is so that your capacity can be stretched to embrace new realms of greatness. You know that you are not satisfied with your life. Many of you have settled in a small place. You know you were born for more and that you have the potential to produce so much more. I was tired of playing it safe. I was tired of living with self-imposed lids and limitations. I was tired of letting ceilings and barriers exist in my life. The inner prompting forced me to embrace a life of no limitations and no boundaries. I silenced fear and started living from the realm of faith. I started shattering ceilings, crossing boundaries, pioneering new territories and conquering new frontiers. Essentially, it was the inner prompting that awakened me to what I was born for. Elisha did not allow the field to become a place of mediocrity but instead a place of motivation, momentum, mastery and the maximization of his potential. Elisha did not shrink his vision to fit the field. No, Elisha elevated his vision and stretched his faith. Elisha stretched to such a point that he no longer saw the field. Elisha saw himself in his prophetic future and fulfilling his prophetic assignment. Stop allowing the field to lie to you and start letting your faith become the currency that makes your future your present reality. You are not going to live another day of your life defined by the spirit of containment. You are being prompted from within to make a significant contribution in your generation and lifetime. You can stop wondering if there is more to life. I am letting you know that there is more to your life and you can manifest more. When you close your ears to fear you can start to see through the eyes of faith.

The field was a place of capacity building in the life of Elisha. It is one thing to know that you were made for more. On the other hand, it is another thing to reach for more in your life. Your life is always a reflection of what you have the courage to reach for. So I want to stop and ask you a very important question: what will you have the courage to reach for in your lifetime? Will you reach for average and mediocrity? Will you accept the status quo? Honestly, it does not take much effort or require much energy to live an ordinary life. Consequently, you will always have to exert energy to elevate your life to the next level. New realms are never accessed without having the courage to reach for more. The person that settles for average will allow the field to become a place of contentment. What I have discovered over the years is that when you settle in the place of contentment you stop contending. Additionally, contentment is the mother of containment which ultimately results in a crippled life. Elisha was not content and he was willing to contend for his prophetic destiny. Therefore, Elisha was willing to understand that you will never realize more for your life until you dare to reach for more. Elisha was willing to reach beyond the limiting circumstances in his life and reach for limitless capacity. Elisha, moved with prophetic impetus and apostolic thrust, married his prophetic future and divorced the field. Elisha used the currency of faith to reach into the realm of the spirit and to pursue a reality that was unborn in time. In other words, Elisha reached beyond the confines of his circumstances and realized the unlimited capacity that he possessed to fulfill his calling. Elisha no longer saw the field as a place that contained him but as a catalyst into everything he had been created for. Elisha tapped into the mind of God and perceived that which was not yet born in time. Inner promptings are a prophetic catalyst into the infinite possibilities of what your life can become. Reaching is not a passive activity. Reaching is a persistent and passionate pursuit. Reaching is growing and developing to such a point that you grasp your prophetic destiny. We do not have enough reachers in this generation. Many people have become restricted by the field. Yet, not many have allowed the field to empower them to reach their prophetic futures. The field was never intended to be a place of regret. The field is a resource designed to empower you to realize your full potential. The field is God's way of growing you so you can grasp the magnitude of the assignment on your life. That is why I can look back in retrospect and see that my difficulties were pregnant with diamonds, my pressure is what produced pearls in my life, and my sorrow was the womb by which God birthed me into significance. Adversity is what awakens you to latent talents, abilities and potentialities. I can truly say that the field is what trained me to thrive. If you erase the field you ultimately erase my future. The field is where God molds you for more. The field matures you to fulfill the mission of your life. Stop seeing the field as a limitation in your life and see it as the key to lifting you into new realms of possibilities and opportunities.

Honor

Honorable Living Exercises

1. Are you cursing cycles in your life?

2. Do you have a clear vision for your life?

3. Are you deploying the strategy of prophetic warfare and fighting for your future?

4. Are you sensitive to the inner promptings and stirrings?

5. What are you reaching for in your life?

CHAPTER 3: THE INVITATION TO GREATNESS

"We are all invited into greatness but very few people are willing to make the investments to manifest greatness."
-Jamelle Sanders

19 So Elijah went and found Elisha son of Shaphat plowing a field. There were twelve teams of oxen in the field, and Elisha was plowing with the twelfth team. Elijah went over to him and threw his cloak across his shoulders and then walked away. 20 Elisha left the oxen standing there, ran after Elijah, and said to him, "First let me go and kiss my father and mother good-bye, and then I will go with you!"
Elijah replied, "Go on back, but think about what I have done to you."
21 So Elisha returned to his oxen and slaughtered them. He used the wood from the plow to build a fire to roast their flesh. He passed around the meat to the townspeople, and they all ate. Then he went with Elijah as his assistant. -1st Kings 19:19-21

Greatness is a word that we throw around so loosely these days. However, I am not sure that many people have a clue what it takes to produce a life of greatness. I believe that every human being on this planet is given an invitation to manifest greatness in their lifetime. Unfortunately, most people are not willing to put in the work that it takes to produce a life of greatness. Many people will read this simple text of scripture and find it quite ordinary. However, I read this text and I find it pregnant with prophetic truths and insights that have the power to revolutionize the way we live. Elisha had spent many years working in the family business. We find him in this text plowing with twelve yoke of oxen. Nothing about that sounds fun or exciting. However, it was the family business and I am sure that the family was thrilled about the prospect of Elisha taking over the business and continuing the family name and legacy. The family had big plans for Elisha but God had a masterplan for Elisha that would blow their minds. I want you to do something for me. I want you to stop cursing your destiny because the conditions in your life presently do not look desirable. We have already established that greatness is often hidden in obscurity. We have discussed the importance of the field to your prophetic future. Now we turn our attention to the invitation to a life of greatness.

Elisha had devoted his life to the field and was destined to be at the head of the family business. I am sure in the community that many people had already prophetically scripted his destiny and they saw him taking on the role of the CEO of the family business.

Every single time he was seen in the community, I am sure that people were prophesying that this is who is going to ensure the succession of the oxen business. No matter what has been declared over your life you must never forget that there is only one thing that you have been destined to do. Never allow what others attempt to name you to negotiate your prophetic destiny. While the field may have attempted to define Elisha, the field was simply God's way of deploying Elisha for prophetic destiny. In other words, where you are presently may not be where God has assigned you. Understand that obscurity is not a barrier to greatness in your life. What I have learned over three decades of living is that obscurity is the birthing canal for greatness in your life. We live in a world that has trained us to despise a small beginning. Zechariah 4:10 instructs us to "do not despise these small beginnings, for the LORD rejoices to see the work begin, to see the plumb line in Zerubbabel's hand." In other words, it is not about where you start but it is ultimately about how you finish. While the beginning for Elisha may appear to be small, the same field is where God would birth significance in his life. Refuse to allow the field of development to define you or detain you. Your field is shaping you to step into the significance of what you were made for. However, if your context of the field is wrong then you will curse your future. Refuse to live as a captive to the field and allow it to serve as the catalyst that unlocks your prophetic future. While your today may look contrary to the tomorrow that you have dreamed of, you must understand that your field is God's training ground for you reigning in life. If you will learn to embrace the training, then you will be empowered to thrive and create a life of total victory.

Elisha had been sensing and feeling that he was born for more and destined for more. As a prophetic intercessor, Elisha had been picking up prophetic promptings and stirrings. Elisha had prophetic acumen and acuity and he was sensitive to the fact that his season was getting ready to change. Elisha did not have all the details but he had discernment that a defining moment was getting ready to happen in his life. This is why Elisha was able to persevere even when his present reality did not match his prophetic destiny. Elisha was able to faithfully cultivate his field because he knew that he was getting ready to have a collision with his prophetic destiny. Elisha was not living with a toxic or escapism mentality. No, Elisha had cultivated possibility thoughts and he was expectant of the shifting of his season. Elisha was anticipating the day when he would activate his prophetic destiny. All the preparation and planting was getting ready to produce a massive harvest in his life. Elisha had done the work to be presented with an invitation to greatness. We have too many people now expecting greatness with no investments. It is illegal to expect a return without an investment ever being made. You have to stop coveting lifestyles that you refuse to pay the cost to produce. We have to stop envying those that have expanded their capacity and embraced life at the next level. Elisha did not have idle seasons in his life. Elisha was investing in a reality that was not yet born in time. Elisha was sowing for a season of significance and greatness in his life. When he had the opportunity to faint and lose heart, Elisha had a prophetic portrait of what was possible for his life. Elisha was willing to fight for the prophetic fulfillment of that which he had seen.

One day Elisha was plowing like he had always done but it was something different about this day. This was the day when heaven and earth conspired to prosper him. This was what I call a tipping point or a defining moment in his life. While Elisha is plowing with the twelve yoke of oxen, the senior prophet Elijah comes and lays his mantle on Elisha and then walks away. Notice that Elijah spoke no words, made no grand announcements, or even acknowledged Elisha. All Elijah did was place the mantle on his shoulders and walk away. All the days of laboring and toiling in the field had created enough friction in the realm of the spirit to bring Elisha into prophetic fulfillment. All the obscurity was aligning Elisha for prophetic opportunity. All the discomfort was serving as a catalyst to his divine appointment. The day that Elisha had been sensing and feeling for quite some time had finally arrived. Elijah simply presented Elisha with an opportunity to choose a different life. Elisha had been born for more but now the mantle for more had shown up in his life. Was he really ready to pursue more in his life? Or would he settle for living among the clutter of the common? Elisha was being presented with an opportunity to advance and ascend into new realms of power and influence. Elisha was being given the opportunity to say goodbye to the past and hello to his prophetic destiny.

The mantle had been placed on his shoulders and Elisha was presented with a decision. Was he going to shoulder a new mantle and anointing? Or was he going to settle for mediocrity and average? What I have discovered is that oftentimes we say that we want to leave the field but we linger in the field. The reason we linger is because we often choose to marry the field and we never marry the future. A future that you refuse to marry will only create moments of frustration and failure in your life. You must be willing to divide yourself from everything that stands in the way of your prophetic destiny. Elisha had an important decision to make. Was he going to stay and run the family business? Or was he going to embrace his Kingdom assignment and mantle? We must always understand that on the heels of every major transition in our lives we will be faced with the question of settling for what is familiar or seizing the future. Elijah cast the mantle on Elisha as an invitation to embrace a brand new way of living. The greatest enemy to a new season in your life is the failure to walk out of the old season. Transition often creates tension in our lives. This tension is created because we are often uncomfortable with the unknown. If you want what you have never had, then you must be willing to do what you have never done before. In other words, the invitation to greatness in your life will often come with illogical instructions. Transition will always test your devotion to your prophetic destiny. When the mantle was placed on the shoulders of Elisha he realized that he was being presented with an invitation. Invitations are either accepted or rejected. Elisha had to make the decision that his destiny was more important to him than his history. A new way of living would require a new way of thinking.

Many of you reading this book are at a crossroads in your life. You know that you were made for more and that you have been destined for greatness. However, many of you are afraid of the great unknown. Too often we risk forfeiting the future for the reassurance of what is familiar and convenient in our lives. However, you have to understand that you will never flourish in the place of familiarity. God will always call you out of the familiar and into a land that is foreign to you. God sends us into foreign places to develop our faith. Your potential cannot be realized in a restricted place. As long as you cling to the old you will never qualify for the new in your life. Just like Elisha you are being presented with an invitation to greatness. In fact, every person on this planet is being presented with the invitation to greatness. It is what you do with the invitation that determines if you maximize your potential and manifest greatness in your lifetime and generation. Elijah cast the mantle on Elisha and walked away. In other words, Elisha had to be tested in his loyalties. Divided loyalties will destroy your legacy. Elisha had to decide if he was going to be loyal to his history or his destiny. Many of you are probably saying that he should be loyal to his destiny. However, I want to ask you a very important question: are you being loyal to your destiny? When the invitation to embrace greatness shows up in your life, are you making excuses to stay small or are you embracing significance and greatness? Your loyalty reveals what you love and will define the level that you live from. Make sure that you are not more loyal to a season than you are to the seed of potential that resides on the inside of you. To decline the invitation to greatness is to be denied destiny. Never choose a season of memories over a season of manifestation in your life. Are you truly invested in your greatness? You will be tested in your commitment to the fulfillment of your purpose and the maximization of your potential. Elisha was not purposed for the field. Elisha's purpose was to be a prophetic voice to nations. However, Elisha's decision was going to decide his destiny. I do not think that enough people truly understand this. Otherwise, we would stop sacrificing tomorrow for the temporary pleasures of today. You have been extended an invitation into greatness. However, your decisions are deciding your future. It is not enough to know that more is possible for your life. Greatness will never manifest in your life until you understand that more has to be pursued. Often times we perceive that more is possible for our lives. However, we are unwilling to pursue the more that is possible. Your life is the product of your pursuits. Your pursuits are a reflection of your priorities. If Elisha did not prioritize his time in the field, he would have never qualified to pursue his prophetic future. Investments require time, energy and risks. Your tolerance for risks will determine the rewards that you experience in your life. When Elijah laid the mantle on Elisha, this was a prophetic announcement that the future had just shown up. Elijah represented the future or prophetic fulfillment of that which had been destined. When that which has been destined for your life shows up will you have the courage to detach from that which has tried to define you? Or will you defer the opportunity and choose to live your life detained to the field?

When your future walks right by you will you say hello to tomorrow and goodbye to today? Elijah represented what was possible for Elisha. Elijah represented the end of a season and the beginning of a new era in the life of Elisha. Elijah did not need to utter a word. After all, God had spoken precisely to Elijah that Elisha was the next emerging prophetic voice and that he was to anoint him for this new assignment in his life. Furthermore, Elisha was a prophetic intercessor and he had been praying and plowing in prayer. He knew that his season was shifting and the tide was turning in his life. Elisha understood that he was at the brink of a breakthrough and the dawning of a new day in his life. However, as you have heard me say many times before, moments have to be perceived before they can be seized. Was Elisha aware of the magnitude of the moment and the opportunity that was presenting itself to him? Did Elisha understand that the greatest prophetic voice of that time had just cast his mantle on him and walked away? Was Elisha truly convinced that God had called him? Did Elisha realize how much God favored him that we would send the prophet Elijah to visit him in the field? As I often say, you never have to wonder if God loves you because He will always locate you. Nor do you have to question if God favors you because He will always find you. God found Elisha in his field and presented him with the opportunity to fulfill his prophetic destiny. Elisha had been extended an incredible opportunity and he had some big decisions to make. Destiny will often present you with prophetic intersections. These are moments where you have to make the choice to step into greatness or to settle for good enough. Do not let your future walk away from you without you having the courage to embrace it. Greatness will be forfeited in your life unless you are willing to greet your future.

Elijah does not find himself in just any field. Elijah finds himself in the field of the next prophetic voice and history shaper. Elijah knew what Elisha was destined for. However, he also understood that Elisha had to be ready to embrace the next realm in his life. Elisha had been in the field for years praying and dreaming of the day when he would step into his prophetic destiny. As some of you can attest to, we have a tendency to limit our date with destiny to some distant moment in the future. What we fail to realize is that destiny is a moment that must be perceived in your life. It is one thing to be aware that your life has great potential. On the other hand, it is a completely different thing to be awakened to the potential that lies on the inside of you. Elijah casting that mantle on Elisha was an activation of his prophetic destiny. This is what Elisha had been hoping, dreaming and praying for. What Elisha did not understand is that responsibility is what ushers you into the next realm. For many years, Elisha had been responsible for the oxen in the field. Now Elisha was responsible for owning a moment and stepping into his prophetic future. Years of development were getting ready to culminate into prophetic destiny. Elisha had been invited into the realm of greatness. This was his opportunity to prove that his destiny was his priority and his history was only a memory. Would he let this moment slip or would this moment be seized in his life? Elisha was pregnant with potential and prophetic promise. However, Elisha now needed new relationships to usher him into new realms.

The invitation to greatness is very exciting and extremely expensive. Your capacity will die in confined places. Conversely, your true capacity emerges when you shatter ceilings and limitations. Elisha had been called to greatness but now it was time to covenant with greatness in his life. In other words, it is not enough for you to have a picture of what is possible for your life. You must also be willing to partner with what is possible for your life. Today's death is what will ultimately give birth to tomorrow's dreams. Your potential is massive but you must have the audacity to pursue more for your life. Elijah represented a season of change in Elisha's life. A new day will require you to make new decisions. You know that a bigger life is beckoning you. Deep down inside you know that you cannot stay small. You have been destined to live a life of significance. Stop saying one day and understand that all it takes is the perception of one moment to change the trajectory of your life forever. When what you were born for arrives then where you have been becomes completely irrelevant. Elijah represented tomorrow. Your tomorrow does not have to look anything like your today. Your faithfulness to the field has been preparing you to step into the fullness of your mission. You have been invited into greatness but you must dare to say yes. You must dare to silence the lies that you are unworthy and to step into the great unknown. You must refuse to doubt and second guess yourself. Everything in your life has been preparing you for this moment. The moment that you realize that seed of greatness that lives within you. The moment that you awaken to the fact that what is in you is so much greater than what is going on around you. So that you can realize like Elisha that someday has become today and that your destiny is right now. You have been invited into greatness. So your days of living in the league of the ordinary are over. The mantle has been cast, the invitation to greatness has been extended and now you must choose destiny.

What you want most will determine whether or not you manifest greatness. Too often we choose the here and now over the destined and ordained. What we fail to realize is that invitations do not always present themselves to us again. What you do with an invitation will determine the height of your success or the gravity of your failure. I want you to really listen to me for a moment. You are not just reading a book. I am speaking to you prophetically right now. I have seen far too many people waste opportunities and reject invitations over the years. Over the years, I have heard people say I have all the time in the world. Also, some people believe that seasons come back around. As someone that knows about the power of seasons and moments, I can tell you that some seasons and moments never come back around. Ephesians 5:16 says "redeeming the time, because the days are evil." In other words, you have to make the most of the opportunities that come your way. Stop believing the lie that you have all the time in the world. Honestly, all you have is this moment right now. What you do with this moment will determine if you maximize your potential or manifest a life of mediocrity. You must discern destiny moments in your life. You must take advantage of the invitation that has been extended to you.

The most prevailing question that life is constantly asking us is this: what do you really want? As Elisha comes face to face with the possibility of a new beginning in his life, he is faced with a very important decision. Will he choose to believe that the field is the place of destiny? Or will he perceive an invitation to greatness in his life? Elisha was gifted with a blank page. The invitation to greatness is the opportunity to create a new story and write new chapters in your life. The invitation to greatness is the opportunity to script a new reality filled with limitless possibilities and opportunities. More importantly, the invitation to greatness is the opportunity to grow the seed of your potential, find new meaning in your life and embrace a new mantle. The casting of a mantle is always the catalyst for new moments in your life. Elijah showed up ushering Elisha into a new day in his life. A day of destiny, dreams fulfilled and divine appointments. Your destiny is always calling you and your history has nothing important to say to you. When destiny calls make the decision to answer the call. Your future is not loud or boisterous. Your future has no need to compete with the noise in your life. Elijah did not even have to open his mouth. All Elijah had to do was show up and cast the mantle. The casting of the mantle was the announcement that Elisha was next. When God tags you then everything else takes a backseat to your new tomorrow. Elisha went to bed believing that a new day was possible for his life and woke up with an invitation to step into a new day. Elisha qualified for promotion because he had made room for more in his life. When you make room for more you become a magnet for success and prosperity. Investments define the increase of your life. Elisha had made such great investments in the field that he had made room for increase in his future. The same field that had the potential to restrict him is the same field that rewarded him and released him into prophetic destiny.

Honorable Living Exercises

1. What have you allowed to name you and negotiate your prophetic destiny?

2. Are you discerning defining moments in your life?

3. What are you doing with your invitation to greatness?

4. Will you dare to leave the familiar and embrace new frontiers?

5. How will you honor the blank page in your story of greatness?

Part 2:

Development

"Development of your capacity is
proof that you
honor the seed of your potential."
-Jamelle Sanders

CHAPTER 4: RECKLESS ABANDONMENT

"Anything that you refuse to abandon will
stifle the advancement of your life."
-Jamelle Sanders

19 So Elijah went and found Elisha son of Shaphat
plowing a field. There were twelve teams of oxen in
the field, and Elisha was plowing with the twelfth
team. Elijah went over to him and threw his cloak
across his shoulders and then walked away. 20 Elisha
left the oxen standing there, ran after Elijah, and said
to him, "First let me go and kiss my father and mother
good-bye, and then I will go with you!"
Elijah replied, "Go on back, but think about what I
have done to you."
21 So Elisha returned to his oxen and slaughtered
them. He used the wood from the plow to build a fire
to roast their flesh. He passed around the meat to the
townspeople, and they all ate. Then he went with
Elijah as his assistant. -1st Kings 19:19-21

If you have been following this text, we just
finished talking about the invitation to greatness. I
spoke at length about how every human being on this
planet is presented with an invitation to greatness.
Unfortunately, most people reject that invitation
because they are not willing to make investments to

improve the quality of their lives. You will never advance in life without making quality investments. Also, you are always investing in something. When you invest in that which is unprofitable you produce unfruitful seasons in your life. One of the greatest enemies to the possibilities of your life is living imprisoned to your past. I see people every single day that cannot be present because they have decided to live imprisoned to the past. The reality is that every single moment of our lives we are choosing bondage or freedom. You cannot afford to hold on to the past at the expense of your prophetic destiny. Yet the past is the thing that holds most people back and robs them of the possibilities of what their lives can become. In this text, we find Elisha about to make the exact same mistake. Elijah had just cast his mantle on Elisha and presented him with the opportunity to walk out of the old and into the new. Elisha had been feeling this dissatisfaction with his life. Dissatisfaction is a prophetic announcement that you are being called to the next dimension. It is sad that many people cannot go up higher because they are still being held hostage by their history. At some point, you must be willing to let go of your history in order to embrace your prophetic destiny. What you are unwilling to say goodbye to will hijack the growth and greatness of your life. You must make a decision about whether you will live your life as a slave to your past or a servant to your purpose. The great divide between your history and destiny can only be closed with a quality decision. Your decisions decide your future and define the fulfillment or failure of your life. Many of you are at a great divide in your life right now. You must make the decision of whether you are going to live chained to your past or catapulted into new possibilities and opportunities for your life. The quality of your decisions shapes the quest of your prophetic destiny.

Elisha had spent a lifetime dreaming of a different life. Housed in him was the capacity to believe for more, press for more, and produce more. However, capacity without choice will only cripple your life. Notice that even after the invitation from the senior prophet Elijah we still find Elisha in an inner war. Elisha hesitated and said that he wanted to go tell his mother and father goodbye. Many people will read over this and miss the profound insights and revelation in this text. Elisha's parents represented his history. While it was admirable for him to want to say goodbye to his family, we must also understand that the family represents what is familiar and comfortable in our lives. Elisha was wrestling with the decision to leave the comforts of the familiar to chart the course into unknown frontiers. When Elisha made the statement that he wanted to say goodbye to his parents, Elijah tells Elisha to go back and think about what just happened in his life. In other words, Elijah was telling Elisha that you cannot afford to miss your destiny because it is different and producing discomfort. You cannot give up the promise of a God-ordained future for the pleasure of present-day security. At some point in your life, you will have to make the decision that security is not more important than significance, comfort is not more important than capacity, and that fear is not worth sabotaging your prophetic future. Elisha was at war on the inside and it was getting ready to influence the decisions that would shape his world. The destiny that Elisha had prayed, sowed, and planted for was in jeopardy of being forfeited because of fear. Elisha was going to have to unleash courageous faith in order to conquer new frontiers in his life. Elisha was not going to be released to step into a new season until he was first willing to settle the issues of his destiny.

I want to take my time with this text for a moment. Many of you are anxious to read on and see what other insights I am going to share. However, I want to speak with you prophetically for a moment. You picked up this book because you are in a transition in your life. You want more and you know that you have been wired for more. You are tired of mediocrity and maintaining the status quo. You are ready to push the boundaries of your potential and release the greatness within you. The problem is that you are stuck, stagnant, and stifled. You want to embrace your tomorrow but you are not willing to let go of your yesterday. Honestly, there are some things about your old season that you still like. There are relationships, passions, appetites, habits, desires, and even attachments to the old season that you are unwilling to let go of. You are in what I call a season of decision. A season of decision is when you must make the choice between what your life once was and what your life can become. The familiar will always war against your future. More importantly, memories will always challenge new moments in your life. Your new life is going to cost you your old one and too many people do not want to let go of the old life. Every time you look back you limit who you can become. Furthermore, when we look back it is proof positive that we are choosing our history over our destiny. New chapters will never be written until you are first willing to let go of old circumstances. In order to choose destiny, you have to stop holding on to what was and dare to embrace what God has for you. I have seen too many people that are living as slaves to memories and they cannot seize moments. Do not waste the treasure of time rehashing yesterday at the expense of your tomorrow.

You will never embrace a new season until you sever your attachment to old seasons and cycles in your life. We like our bondage because we have built our lives on it. Everything about us has been developed based on our dysfunctions. Most people have no clue how to live from a place of liberation. When I truly made the decision that I was going to fulfill my purpose and maximize my potential, I had to settle the issues of my destiny. In other words, I had to make a non-negotiable decision about what I was no longer going to tolerate in my life. I had to silence the lies, surrender the inadequacies, deal with the defects, and totally detach from my past in order to embrace my prophetic destiny. You have to settle the what-ifs in your mind in order to walk in your true identity and own your personal power. You have to stop allowing social impediments, psychological buttons, emotional triggers, labels, stigmas, trauma, and emotional blackmail to control your life. You have to be willing to die to your history to discover your prophetic destiny. You cannot carry any residue of the old into the new season of your life. You have to be willing to break cycles and create brand new chapters in the story of your life. Settling the issues of your destiny is not about suppression. Settling the issues of your destiny will require the surrendering of the old in order to be solidified in the new. You cannot take half of yourself into your future. You can only take your healed self into your future. In other words, settling the issues of your destiny is changing your story so you can change your season.

Some people will say that Elijah was harsh and rude with Elisha. However, mentors understand that reckless abandonment is required to embrace your assignment. In fact, I often say that reckless abandonment is the price of entry into the next season of your life. If you have followed my work over the years, then you have heard me talk about reckless abandonment before. However, I am sure you have never heard me talk about it at this length. Reckless abandonment is not just walking away from your former life but it is fearlessly embracing your new life. Reckless abandonment is being willing to say goodbye to the old you in order to embrace the brand new you. Reckless abandonment does not happen without resolve. Furthermore, reckless abandonment is the resolve to renounce everything that restricts and robs you of a rich and meaningful life. Elijah knew that if Elisha was not resolved then he would be robbed of the invitation to greatness. Resolve is possessing the fortitude to leave the familiar and embrace your future. Reckless abandonment is being willing to wave goodbye to everything that wars against God's greater plan and purpose for your life. Reckless abandonment is the willingness to divorce your past in order to discover, cultivate, and maximize your greatest potential. Ultimately, reckless abandonment is dying to your agenda to discover God's assignment for your life. Reckless abandonment is the death of your history for the life of your destiny. Not many people are willing to say goodbye to the past to realize their greatest potential. The choice to walk away from your history is what awakens you to your prophetic destiny.

Elisha was wrestling between his old life and the new life that was waiting on him. What most people fail to understand is that every change in life is connected to a choice. More importantly, connected to every choice is a course that our lives take. Elisha was going back to hug his history. I would imagine it would be difficult for Elisha to leave the family. After all, he was an heir to the oxen company and his life had already been planned out. Elisha was going to take over the family business and everyone had big plans for Elisha's life. Now God is telling Elisha to leave everything that is familiar to him and embrace his prophetic future. The moment a decision is made destiny is influenced. Elisha knew that this was a big decision. It is one thing to sense more for your life. On the other hand, it is another thing to seize the more that is available to you. It is in seasons of decision that we seize our destinies. At that moment, Elisha was thinking about everything that he was giving up. Elisha was leaving his family, leaving a stable career, leaving his inheritance, and leaving his investment. In fact, it is almost impossible to walk away from something that you are invested in. Elijah said something so profound and I do not think that many people really understand the gravitas of what he said. Elijah told him to go back and think about what he had done to him. In other words, ponder your path and perceive the prophetic opportunity that has been presented to you. While the words may seem harsh to some, Elijah knew that at that moment Elisha had to choose between his history and his destiny. Whatever decision he made would influence his destiny forever. Elijah had already allowed frustration to manipulate his own future. So he knew that making an emotional choice would have eternal consequences. Elisha had to determine how bad he wanted his destiny. Until you want your destiny bad enough to divorce the past, you will never discover your true purpose in life.

It was vitally important that Elisha discerned the season he was in. Why was this so important? Your discernment of seasons determines the significance of your life. Additionally, your discernment of seasons defines your success. The most important thing you must understand is that discerning seasons is how your destiny is shaped. The hesitation soon subsided and Elisha gave his history the gift of goodbye. Do you really want to be great? Are you serious about your destiny? How bad do you want to live at the next level? What you are willing to say goodbye to will determine what you say hello to. Elisha was willing to say goodbye to his history and hello to his prophetic destiny. Elisha dared to say goodbye yesterday and hello to a new today in his life. You will never manifest greatness until you are willing to give yourself the gift of goodbye. You have lived a lifetime of grief because of things you refused to say goodbye to. Now set yourself free by giving yourself the gift of goodbye. Say goodbye to the misery and the memories. Say goodbye to frustration and failure. The gift of goodbye is being willing to sever and separate from everything that stands between you and the next season of your life. The gift of goodbye is maturing to the point where you realize some things do not belong in your life because they do not serve who you were born to be. Old garments will never fit a new season in your life. When you try to move forward without removing what you have outgrown, it becomes opposition to the next season of your life. Face the fact that some things no longer fit you.

Elisha then returns to the oxen. What? Did he decide to stay? Did he choose his history over his destiny? No, Elisha returned to the oxen not to say hello to his former self at the expense of his future self. Elisha returned to the oxen as a prophetic announcement and a prophetic demonstration. Elisha gave himself the gift of goodbye by not just surrendering his past but slaughtering his past. In other words, Elisha was willing to slay the thing that once brought him significance. Elisha violently destroyed everything that stood in the way of his victory. Elisha demolished everything that tried to define and detain him. What are you willing to slaughter to embrace a new season in your life? Elisha was courageous because he was willing to slaughter everything that attempted to make him second guess the new season in his life. Elisha did not hold on so tightly to his history that he could not embrace his destiny. In other words, Elisha was not willing to compromise on anything that God was circumcising out of his life. While slaughtering is a painful action, it empowered Elisha to partner with his Kingdom assignment. Elisha allowed what attempted to label him to liberate him to step into the magnitude of his calling. If you keep reading, Elisha did not stop with simply slaughtering the oxen but he went on to burn the oxen. This brings me to the point that some things have to be burned out of your life in order for you to become who you were born to be. Elisha was willing to destroy the memory of everything that stood in the way of his destiny moment. Elisha was so invested in his destiny that the connection to his history was irreconcilable. In other words, Elisha did not want any trace of his history to produce a tethering of his destiny. Elisha died to his old life and made the decision to embrace his prophetic destiny. Elisha understood that if he burned the oxen that he would have nothing to go back to. If there was no point of return then he would have no premise for regret in his life. As long as you cleave to the pieces of your history, you will never partner with your prophetic destiny. Elisha abandoned everything he ever knew to embrace a Kingdom assignment that offered him no guaranteed rewards. Elisha was willing to abandon everything to awaken to the Kingdom. What you are willing to walk away from will always determine what you access. Elisha understood that sacrifice was a seed that heaven could not refuse. Sacrifice was stretching him to step into his next.

The text goes on to say that Elisha feeds the family and the town before he leaves. I find it remarkable that this young emerging prophet never resented his place of development. In fact, even upon his departure, the region is being strengthened by his sacrifice. The seed of your life should nourish every environment that you enter. Elisha nourishes a community that did not have the capacity to discern or perceive his next. In other words, even in his exit, he is still empowering the place of his development. Elisha did not leave the field barren or unfruitful. Elisha left the field fully maximizing the season. Are you maximizing your season? Can your contributions strengthen and sustain your community? Have you worked your field to such a point that entire regions can feast and harvest from your sacrifices? Elisha did not leave his region empty. Elisha left his region empowered. Through service and sacrifice, he demonstrated what it means to be devoted to your field. While Elisha was working the field, God was working out the details of his future. Once his history was closed, Elisha made the bold decision to step into his future. Elisha burns the oxen as a powerful prophetic demonstration. Burning the oxen was reprogramming his mind so that he had no more options but to partner with prophetic destiny. Elisha trusted that saying goodbye to the past was the seed for saying hello to a brand new tomorrow. Your today does not have to look anything like your yesterday. Wave goodbye to yesterday and dare to walk into greatness!

The greatest gift you can give yourself is the gift of goodbye. Your past cannot speak without your permission. Yesterday cannot rule you without you yielding. History cannot enslave the soul that is healed. Yesterday is history, today is a memory and tomorrow is not yet born to time. You do not have to live another day of your life on stutter and stuck in old seasons and cycles. You can end cycles of regret right now by renewing your mind to your true identity and nature. Say goodbye to toxic thoughts, toxic emotions, and distorted perceptions. Say goodbye to insecurity, inferiority, and inadequacy. Say goodbye to every lie and limitation that has made you feel worthless and insignificant. Refuse to allow a horrible past to rob you of an incredible future. Elisha dared to silence the past and seize the possibilities of what his life could become. Giving yourself the gift of goodbye is eliminating every threat to transition and transformation in your life. When Elisha burned the oxen, he made a prophetic declaration that what had been predestined for him was more important than the prison of the past. Finally, remember that freedom is the gateway to your future. Goodbye is always the catalyst that unleashes God's best in your life.

Goodbye is not the ending of your life. Goodbye empowers you to embrace your greatest existence. Give yourself the gift of goodbye so you can say hello to your future!

Honorable Living Exercises

1. Will you live as a slave to your past or a servant of your purpose?

2. Are you afraid to leave the familiar in order to embrace your future?

3. Do you have the courage to settle the issues of your destiny?

4. What do you need to recklessly abandon?

5. Are you ready to give yourself the gift of goodbye?

"You cannot create authentic success without
possessing a servant's heart."
-Jamelle Sanders

When you mention the word servant in the
presence of most people, you will get snarls, eye rolls
and other condescending looks. We live in a time
where the word servant has taken on a negative
connotation. In fact, many people see it as a form of
slavery and bondage. Most people react to the word
servant as if it is an obscene or profane word. I think
this is one of the reasons that many people never rise
to their full potential or experience a life of success
and prosperity. We live in an era where people think
that leadership is power, manipulation, and control.
However, leadership is service and you will never
succeed in leadership until you see it from this
perspective. Matthew 23:11 states "But he that is
greatest among you shall be your servant." In this
very short verse of scripture, Jesus makes it clear that
Kingdom greatness is only obtained through
servanthood. So for those that may be still confused, I
want to make it very practical for you. Leadership is
not defined by your title, position, education, pedigree
or historicity. Leadership is defined and deeply rooted

in service. Without a servant's heart, you will never truly live a life of significance. This is one of the greatest challenges that I see in leadership today. Everyone is trying to make it to the top but nobody wants to serve. The problem with this model is that if everyone wants to be served and nobody wants to serve then someone becomes unnecessary. It is vitally important that servanthood is the foundation of your leadership.

All my life I have been left out and looked over. I was never the popular one and I did not quite fit into the in-crowd. I have always found myself behind the scenes often taking on the roles and doing the responsibilities that nobody else wanted to do. I have never had a problem with being in the background. I did not mind cleaning toilets, mopping floors, taking out the trash and all the other tasks that many find menial. However, when I look at the landscape of leadership today I do not see a lot of people that share my sentiments. I see a lot of people jockeying for positions and fighting to be at the forefront. Unfortunately, I see a lot of people that are reaching for microphones but avoiding service. This is not the hallmark of authentic leadership. This is the hallmark of a performer and we have enough performers living plastic lives and making no real difference in the world. If you want to be a great leader in the twenty-first century then I would challenge you to be willing to go low. What do I mean by going low? It means having a lowly philosophy of power. In other words, it is not thinking less of yourself but thinking of yourself less. It is the ability to lay personal agendas, ambitions, and affections aside to serve a higher purpose. The highest positions in the world require the greatest humility. Jesus was the Son of God and yet He humbles Himself and washes the feet of His disciplines. If the Son of God was able to humble himself in service to humanity, then surely we should be able to serve with humility and honor. Power is not owed to you and we should never forget that leadership is a privilege that we should never take for granted.

As I look around the world today, I see a lack of authentic leadership. Most people lead with an agenda. While they come under the guise of help and service, you quickly discover that personal agendas and personal advancement are the motives. They want to advance and many times they do not care what price they have to pay to ascend. Many times these individuals are charming and charismatic. However, as I have interacted with many of these individuals behind the scenes I quickly discovered that they are artificial, conniving, deceptive, manipulative and they lack strong character. You cannot have a greater affinity for the position than the principles that anchor and authenticate the position. If you have read my book *Chosen*, then you know I speak at length about the challenges of leadership in the twenty-first century. One of the reasons we have seen such a corrosion of leadership is because we have leaders leading with no convictions and no compassion. It is always costly to place someone in a position of leadership that does not care about the people that they lead. I challenge you as you read this book to find yourself in these pages. Evaluate your motives for power. Power without convictions is power that will corrupt. The world does not need any more corrupt leaders. We need leaders of character, morality, honesty and dignity in the twenty-first century. No person with deceptive motives and hidden agendas will take on the role of a servant leader.

Elisha has just left the comforts of home to embrace a future with no guarantees of success. Elisha trusted with unshakable certainty that something great and significant was waiting on the other side of his obedience. Elisha leaves the safety and security of a stable home, career, and family to follow a prophet that he barely even knew. Elisha was getting ready to take over the oxen empire and be the successor to his parents business. Yet God had bigger plans for his life. To some it would seem like a demotion to go from being at the helm of the family business to take on the role of the assistant to Elijah. In fact, if you study further you will learn that Elisha spent most of his time pouring water on the hands of the prophet Elijah and serving as his assistant. I can hear some of you saying that there is no way in the world that you would do that. However, this takes me back to my original point in this chapter about the lack of servanthood in leadership today. Elisha had given up the comforts of home to embrace change and a life that in no way mirrored the life that he had abandoned. More importantly, this new season in his life seems like a demotion from the already planned life that he left at home. I am sure that many of you would have started to complain about this new normal and new reality in your life. Elisha does not complain about it at all. Elisha embraced this new season in his life because he knew that it was pregnant with significance. Elisha did not despise this season of his life because he understood that he was being developed for greatness. More importantly, Elisha understood that no season is insignificant and it all serves as an investment for prophetic destiny.

Elisha knew that God had spoken to him to leave everything that was familiar to him and embrace his prophetic future. Elisha did not waver in the word that he had received from God even when the current context of his life did not seem ideal. Elisha knew that more was available to him. More importantly. Elisha knew that staying home was not honoring the seed of potential on the inside of him. He understood that in order to get to the next level in his life that he was going to have to do something different. While his decision to abandon everything he had ever known was bold, it was also the catalyst that would propel breakthrough in his life. When a mantle is cast moments must be captured to manifest change in your life. Elisha realized that a mantle had been cast on him and that God was inviting him into a new opportunity to expand his horizons, build his capacity, and honor the seed of greatness on the inside of him. Elisha realized that staying safe would only cause him to settle for a second class life. On the other hand, stepping out in faith was the seed that would unlock his prophetic future. Elisha understood that Elijah had the capacity to unlock the seed of potential that was buried deep within him. Therefore, when the mantle was cast Elisha made the decision to embrace mentorship in order to embrace the mantle that was on his life. Elisha did not mind washing the hands of the prophet. Elisha understood that his service to Elijah was the seed for unlocking his capacity for greatness. Furthermore, his service provided the proximity he needed to cultivate the potential that was on the inside of him. The seed of your potential can only be cultivated through your willingness to serve the vision of another person. You cannot receive a mantle from a leader you are unwilling to serve. In fact, without service, the mantle is illegal in your life and you are unauthorized.

Most people today will disregard a message like this. You think you can network and resume shop your way to the top. However, that is not the authentic model for success and advancement. If you really want to get to the top, then you need to learn the towel principle. What is the towel principle? As Jesus humbled himself and washed the feet of His disciples, so you must humble yourself if you want to rise to the place of honor and greatness in the world. The heart of a servant does not desire the microphone. The heart of a servant is to be molded and matured to step into a moment of greatness. A servant does not desire to be praised or applauded. The heart of a servant is always to seek the interest and welfare of others. You know that you do not possess a servant's heart when you are concerned with self-promotion and self-preservation. We have too many people in power that only care about the promotion and preservation of me, myself and I. They lead poorly, they speak sharply and they lack humility. Too many leaders want others to bow down to them when they have never bowed low in service. When you refuse to bow low in service something will break you down and bring you to a place of humility in your life. I want you to stop seeing servanthood as a burden. You must understand that leadership and servanthood is a privilege. In other words, authentic leaders realize that they get to serve. One of the greatest privileges of a lifetime is the opportunity to serve. Servanthood is realizing that it is not about what others can do for you but about what you can do for others.

One of the things that I love about leadership is that I get to serve. The higher up you go the more people you have to serve. Therefore, leadership is not about lording over people but serving people with passion and a pure heart. Pride will cause a person to think that platforms and prestige are the rights of leadership. On the contrary, humility will cause a person to realize that platforms and prominence are rewards of leadership. In other words, when a leader operates in pride they have an entitlement mentality. They think that because they are at the top that others should obey all their commands. These leaders often exercise coercive power over those that they serve. In contrast, servant leaders operate with an empowered mentality. Servant leaders understand that people will only follow leaders that they trust and respect. If you have followed my work over the years, you have heard me say many times that trust is the currency of relationships. Without trust, every relationship in your life will collapse. Ultimately, the difference between prideful leaders and servant leaders is that servant leaders seek the heart of the people and not the hand of the people. In fact, servant leaders understand that without the heart of the people you will never get the help of the people. When you possess a servant's heart, that means that you are willing to get down in the trenches with those that you serve and help make the vision a reality. In fact, leaders should never expect others to do what they are unwilling to do. We have too many people leading with agendas and not leading from a place of authenticity. The world needs empowered leaders that empower their people. When you empower people, you build stronger organizations, communities, families and nations.

Elisha had a servant's heart. Elisha was willing to faithfully serve and pour water on the hands of Elijah. I am sure that some of the students in the school of the prophets probably mocked and ridiculed him. In fact, I can hear them saying things like look at him pouring water on that old man's hands, look at him always following Elijah, or he could be doing so much more with his life. Regardless of the opinions of those around him, Elisha had a word from God and he was not going to let go of it. Elisha continued to serve and assist Elijah in any way that he could. I am sure that some days were difficult, frustrating and unsettling. Yet Elisha continued to serve with a smile and did not complain. Servant leadership is not about what you can get out of it. Servant leadership is about what you can do to enhance the vision and lives of those that you serve. Elisha realized that in his serving he was making the life of Elijah easier. Servanthood empowers you to create strategies, systems, and solutions that empower success. In other words, what others saw as menial God saw as missional. God was using service to shape Elisha into a revolutionary leader that would one day change the world. If Elisha could serve well and maximize the season, God would one day mantle him to step into his season of prophetic fulfillment. As Elisha enhanced the life and ministry of Elijah, God was divinely engineering and empowering Elisha to step into his moment. Elisha was not just pouring water on the hands of the prophet. Elisha was serving the vision of one of the greatest prophets to ever live. Those same hands were performing miracles, signs, and wonders. Not only that, but Elisha was being given the opportunity to see firsthand the global prophetic ministry of Elijah. There is no form of education better than experiential education. Through observation and experience, Elisha was learning from the frontlines the secrets to a thriving and cutting-edge prophetic ministry. Often the power of silent years is that they are pregnant with moments of significance. What seemed like silent years in the life of Elisha was preparing him to one day be a world shaker.

As Elisha poured his life into serving Elijah, God was positioning him to one day step into his prophetic destiny. Servanthood is pouring your life into the service of another man's vision so that one day God can give you your own. In fact, I often say that you are not qualified for promotion until you have lived a life that pours out. What do I mean by a life poured out? A life poured out is a life that is totally invested in the interests, increase, and improvement of the lives of others. A life poured out is a life where you hold nothing back and you give yourself fully to seeing others reach their highest and best potential. A life poured out is a life that is lived selflessly, significantly and servantly. A life poured out is a generous life that gives to others that could never return the favor. I dare you to pursue a life poured out! It was one of the greatest decisions I ever made. It is not about me and I do not even need credit. I live my life for an audience of one. My greatest desire is to hear God say well done. The servant's heart is not about acknowledgment or the accouterments of success. The servant's heart is about the advancement and abounding of the lives of others. Servant leaders understand that when we bow low in service we are empowered to live lives that become a blessing. Leadership is not about the exaltation of self but the extension of service to humanity. The heart of the servant is never vanity but to add value to the lives of others. In everything that I do, I want to uplift, empower and add value to other people's lives. I learned a long time ago that my life is a seed. If I will allow the seed of my life to multiply, then significance is manifested in the lives of many.

There is so much more that I could say about living a life poured out. However, I think that you get the gist of what I was trying to say. I have become so immersed in service that my interest is truly in the progress and prosperity of humanity. I have never made it about me or how I can personally benefit. My heart is to see every person living their greatest life and reaching their greatest potential. I think it is selfish to have a one dimensional perspective of success. The heart of a servant is the betterment of humanity. After all, what is the point of progress if you cannot take others with you? Everything that I have God has given to me. In fact, there is nothing that I have that God did not give me. God is the greatest giver in the world. He broke the world record for the greatest contribution ever given. God gave His only Son in order that we might have eternal life. As a result of God giving the gift of His Son, we have the opportunity to receive a precious gift called eternal life. God giving the gift of His Son was the greatest expression of love. The heart of a servant is to be a demonstration of love in the midst of a world that desperately needs it. Servanthood is not slavery or bondage. Servanthood is the womb of significance. Make the decision to live a life that pours out. Decide today that you will live a life that speaks beyond the grave. Dare to rob the grave of your greatness and to leave a legacy that speaks to generations to come. When you dare to live a life poured out, you are empowered to leave a print on this world that can never be erased. Through service, you have the opportunity to leave an indelible mark on the world that will be recognized by future generations.

Elisha had the heart of a servant. Honestly, most people would have been trying to network, get famous or chase success. However, we find Elisha willing to give it all up to serve the prophet Elijah. Elisha realized that what Elijah carried had the power to change his life and unlock his capacity for greatness. Elisha was willing to bow low in service in order to one day birth a season of significance in his life. Elisha did not shy away from the menial tasks and responsibilities because he realized that it was all molding him for his moment of greatness. Elisha respected Elijah and was willing to follow him even without a guarantee of success and prosperity. Too often we want to skip over service and step right into success. Yet, service is the very thing that will empower your success. If you will find a way to serve humanity, success will become inevitable in your life. Elisha had no agenda and his motives were pure. Some things you need to stop seeing as a demotion in your life and see them as defining moments. Elisha was courageous enough to step away from something he had been promised to embrace what he had been purposed for. Elisha was doing much more than just pouring water on the hands of the prophet Elijah. Elisha was expanding his capacity to embrace a calling not yet born to time. Elisha just continued to pray and pour water on his hands. Elisha did not care how he was perceived. Elisha's willingness to pour water on the hands of Elijah was part of the prophetic plan of God. It placed him in proximity to prophetic destiny. Elisha's service was the seed that was unlocking his prophetic future. The key to going up higher is always humility. Humility is the seed for honor. I want you to understand that leadership is not about how you can be benefited but how can you make the lives of others better. Sacrifice and selflessness reflect the servant's heart. If you want to have sustainable success, then I challenge you to serve with sincerity. We live in a time where imposters are easily exposed. Ascending to the highest heights of success will require authenticity. Power without purity will pervert and we have enough perverted leaders in power. Power with purity is what preserves leadership. Purity will distinguish you in the world. Servanthood will make you rare and cause you to be highly respected in the world.

Honorable Living Exercises

1. Do you possess a servant heart?

2. Can you selflessly serve without the guarantee of a reward?

3. What is your motive for power?

4. Are you willing to be mentored and molded for your moment of greatness?

5. Whose vision have you served in order to one day step into a season of significance in your life?

"Commitment is the great qualifier that ushers
you into the realm of greatness."
-Jamelle Sanders

And it came to pass, when the LORD would
take up Elijah into heaven by a whirlwind,
that Elijah went with Elisha from Gilgal.
-2nd Kings 2:1

As I embarked upon writing this chapter, I was
conflicted about how exactly I could bring all these
concepts together in the most simplistic way. The
concepts in this chapter are very heavy and will
require a few sessions for you to truly excavate the
depth of what I am getting ready to share with you. I
believe that the great connector to a life of success
and prosperity is commitment. As someone that has
mentored and developed leaders around the world,
one of the things that I see missing today is the
principle of commitment. Many people do not have
the right motives for success. I have discovered when
your motives are wrong that you will always sell out
for a counterfeit version of success. If you have read
my book *Significance,* then you know that I write in
great detail about how many people never realize their
greatest potential or manifest greatness because they

can be bought. Most people can be bought because they are broken and dysfunctional in their souls. They do not know who they are or what they possess. When you are unclear about what you possess, you will always sell out for something much less than your significance. If you cannot commit beyond how you can be benefited, then you will never break your way into true success and prosperity. Commitment has to go beyond worldly pleasures and extend to access eternal treasures. If you are only committed based on what you will get out of it, then you will break that commitment the moment that you feel that things are not going in your favor. Can you truly commit even without a guarantee of a reward?

This brings me to a very important point. If I could, I would dissect every single verse in this text and explicate it in great detail. However, that would take two to three more books to fully expound on all the revelation in this text. So I will try and break this down into digestible chunks so you can truly grasp the concepts that I am sharing with you. We see in this text Elijah and Elisha getting ready to leave the place of Gilgal. As I excavated this text and what Gilgal really means, I immediately started to write because this is going to set so many people free. Gilgal literally means a wheel or a rolling away. Now I am sure that some of you are reading this and you do not see the prophetic implications and prophetic significance of this. However, I want to break it down for you a little further. Gilgal is the place where shame is removed and cycles are broken in your life. Elisha had been serving the prophet for years. Elijah was nearing the ending of his ministry. Now, Elisha is being challenged to follow at another level. Moreover, Elisha is being challenged to follow his mentor into a realm that he has never accessed before. In addition, there is no guarantee of a reward or success. Yet Elisha makes the decision to follow the mentor because he believes that his destiny is tied to Elijah. More importantly, Elisha believes that what Elijah carries is essential to him fulfilling his calling. Elisha's willingness to follow was the catalyst to shattering ceilings and unlocking capacity in his life.

Every person that wants to rise to the place of honor will have to go through Gilgal. Many of you reading this book right now are in a Gilgal season in your life. You have lived a lifetime shackled by shame and ruled by regrets. Every single time you have tried to go to the next level, your past has shown up and paralyzed your ability to move forward. You did not pick up this book by accident. In fact, you may have not even thought about reading this book. Yet you decided to open it up and read up until this point. This is my prophetic announcement to you that the shame is getting ready to be removed from your life. Not only that, but the stigma that has been attached to your name is getting ready to be removed from you. Your days of shame, embarrassment and reproach are over. Gilgal is the place where cycles are broken in your life. It is impossible to be a person of honor as long as you are trapped in vicious cycles of frustration, failure, and defeat. Some people are trapped in cycles of victimization, stigmatization, and limitations. Regardless of the type of cycle you are in, I am here to let you know that the cycle can be broken in your life. You can never become who you were born to be as long as you are bound by who you used to be. Every great person must have a Gilgal experience because you must have the courage to walk out of the old and into the new. Cycles are repeated until you have the courage to recognize that you are not going anywhere. Many times people say that they are glad that they are not where they used to be. However, they are also not where they want to be. Where are they exactly? In a cycle going absolutely nowhere. No cycle will ever be broken in your life without a choice. You can either choose to live as a prisoner to your past. Or you can choose to be the prophet of your destiny. Your choices are prophesying your prophetic destiny. If you want to be a person of honor and influence in the world, then it is time to confront the shame and break the cycle. Your voice will always be muted as long as you live victimized by moments. Gilgal is the place where you say goodbye to your former life and you move forward into the incredible destiny that God has for you. Sadly, we have many people that never make it beyond Gilgal. The attachment to the past is so strong that many are never able to align with prophetic destiny. As long as you are held hostage by your past, you cannot honor the seed of your potential. Never allow the mirror of the past to rob you of the miracle of this present moment.

And Elijah said unto Elisha, Tarry here, I pray thee;
for the LORD hath sent me to Bethel. And Elisha said
unto him, As the LORD liveth, and as thy soul liveth,
I will not leave thee. So they went down to Bethel.
- 2nd Kings 2:2

Next, we see that Elijah once again tests the
emerging prophet Elisha. Why did Elijah try to shake
him? Elijah was seeing if Elisha could pass the
commitment test. When you are working on your exit
strategy and succession plan, you better make sure
that you are choosing individuals that have passed the
commitment test. This time Elijah is going to the
region of Bethel. If you study Bethel, you will
discover that it means the house of God. After the
shame is removed and the cycle is broken, then you
come to the house of God. While we have many gurus
and experts in the world today, there is no authentic
success apart from God. I do not care how many
awards, accolades or achievements a person may
have. The absence of God is the absence of greatness.
All greatness finds its origin in God. The reason we
are not seeing great and enduring leadership is
because we have too many people that bought into the
notion that they do not need God. While they may
amass material things, they never possess the eternal
treasure of God on the inside. We are not defined by
our possessions or positions. We are defined by what
we possess on the inside. I watch so many people
chasing after the world's definition of success. Then

they come to me broken, damaged and empty. These individuals quickly discover that their search was all vanity. That they wasted moments and valuable time pursuing things that did not matter. After all, the only essential pursuit is the pursuit of eternity.

Unfortunately, I am greatly disturbed by what I see in the world today. People are jockeying for positions. There is no sincerity and no authenticity. We have people leading who could care less about the people that they lead. We have corrupt and conceited leaders trying to lead organizations and nations into change. While I am a highly respected thought leader with solutions for global problems, I never forget that the foundation of my life is God and apart from Him I will fail. I never get caught up in my influence or my achievements. I realize that I am only succeeding because I am surrendered to God's will and purpose for my life. We have had enough people in leadership that want the position of the leader but not the principles and pillars that anchor the leader. Elijah was sending a strong warning to us about succession planning in leadership. It is not enough to have the title of leader but we need people that can be trusted with the weight of responsibility that comes with leadership. You cannot just have what is on Elijah's life. You have to be willing to get to know the God of Elijah. Elijah was challenging Elisha to go deeper. In other words, Bethel was an invitation to get to know the God that Elijah served. Bethel was the opportunity to follow the senior prophet into the presence of God. It is nothing wrong with admiring the lives of powerful and influential people. However, I want you to understand that there is no authentic success without a spiritual foundation. Many people have ridiculed me over the years for being vocal about my faith. Conversely, I make no apologies for speaking up and speaking out about my faith. I will never seek to force my beliefs on anyone. Nevertheless, I realize that everything I am and everything that I think I have achieved is by the grace of God. I realize that I am not where I am simply because of my education or talent. I realize that I am here because God has chosen me to be a voice of influence in my generation. So I never get conflicted about the fact that I am simply a conduit and that God is the conductor and the source of all power in my life. When the godless lead, the result is apathy, indifference, and a corrupt society. We do not simply need educated leaders. We need leaders that are empowered by God to make a difference in the world. We need leaders that are willing to go to Bethel. Leaders that want to be where God is and leaders that refuse to go unless God goes with them. All great legacies require a Bethel experience. God is the originator of success and succession.

And Elijah said unto him, Elisha, tarry here, I pray thee; for the LORD hath sent me to Jericho. And he said, As the LORD liveth, and as thy soul liveth, I will not leave thee. So they came to Jericho.
-2nd Kings 2:4

As we see in the text, Elijah is once again testing Elisha's commitment. This time the test takes them to Jericho. If you study Jericho, you will realize that it is the place of warfare and the place where walls are crumbled in your life. As someone that has been doing the work for decades, I always tell people that you will never fulfill your destiny without having the courage to fight for your destiny. In fact, I believe that the greatest battle in your life is the battle for destiny. Unfortunately, I have seen too many people lose this battle over the years. Oftentimes we make excuses, we become prisoners to fear, or we simply refuse to fight for the destiny that we know is ours. I want you to listen to me very carefully. You will never fulfill purpose or maximize your greatest potential without encountering intense seasons of spiritual warfare. Warfare will not only test your commitment to your destiny but also your capacity to fulfill your destiny. One thing that I know about warfare is that it demands your undivided attention. If you want to see something disappear in your life, then you simply deprive it of your attention. Whatever you give your attention to you energize and empower. Many are destroyed in seasons of warfare because they are distracted. The cost of a distracted warrior can be deadly. When you sign up for war, you give up the comforts of civilian life. We have too many people trying to enlist in the battle that are still entertaining the affairs of civilian life. As someone that knows a lot about spiritual warfare, I want to be very honest with every recruit that is coming into the Kingdom of God. You cannot serve in God's army without a separation. In other words, when you enlist in the army of God that means that you are under the command and the control of God. It means that you have counted up the cost of war, you have given up the comforts of civilian life, and you have committed to seeing the battle through to the very end. You will never walk in the fullness of your assignment until you are first willing to go to Jericho.

When we talk about spiritual warfare many people have the wrong connotation. Spiritual warfare is not shouting at the enemy and singing warfare songs. Spiritual warfare is the counsel of your mind by any thought, idea, philosophy or suggestion that contradicts the truth of God's word. In other words, the goal of the enemy is to get you to take satanic counsel. Once you take satanic counsel, satanic alliances and confederations are formed and the Spirit is censored in your life. For so long we thought putting on army fatigues and shouting that we were going into the enemy's camp was spiritual warfare. Yet, when we finished singing and shouting our minds were still in bondage to satanic ideologies and philosophies. For too long the church has not realized that the battle is raging for the minds of believers. As a prophetic voice and spiritual neurosurgeon, my assignment is to bring healing and liberation to the minds of God's people so that they can win the war in the soul and ultimately win the war for destiny. A seduced mind is no match for a subtle enemy. As some of you have heard me say before, antiquated thinking will never defeat an advanced enemy. My assignment in the Kingdom is to upgrade the minds of believers to walk in dominion and to manifest the Kingdom in every realm of life.

You don't want to get me started on spiritual warfare. I have heard so many people over the years tell me that they are in spiritual warfare. However, I have learned over three decades that most people are not fighting the devil. Most people are fighting decisions. Since most people are fighting bad decisions, they are no match for the devil. I can tell you about spiritual warfare. I have seen and encountered some things that would make your mouth drop. My mind has come under such satanic attack and demonic assault that I cannot even begin to write about it all here. However, I did not win the war over the enemy by shouting and singing warfare songs. I did not even win the war simply because I came to church. In fact, I sat in church for years and lived a defeated life. I did not win the war over the enemy until I developed and disciplined my mind. An undisciplined mind will never produce an undefeated life. If you want to walk in dominion and authority, then you must become disciplined in your thinking. You have to learn how to take every thought captive and make it obey Christ. As long as you remain undisciplined, you will remain unsuccessful in your warfare. I know this is a little heavy for some people.

Conversely, you have to understand that many times we are prisoners to our thinking. If you never deal with your psychological programming, you will continue to live your life in cycles of frustration, failure and defeat. Until you win the war in your mind, you will never win the war for destiny.

Jericho is a place that many people avoid. Jericho is an uncomfortable place. It is uncomfortable because we have been undisciplined for so long. Too many people have been promoted because we admired their gifts at the expense of their character. Anybody that knows me or has ever worked with me will tell you that I am not fascinated by gifted people. I have watched gifted people self-sabotage and self-destruct. Everyone was fascinated with what they do but nobody ever took the time to confront who they are. In other words, hypocrisy is when what I do and who I am are in conflict with each other. This is a sign that I am not living an authentic life. More importantly, this is a sign of a person that has flaunted their strengths but ignored their weaknesses. Your weaknesses will not only cripple you but also destroy your life. Too many people in positions of leadership have learned how to modify behavior but they have not truly experienced true freedom. The problem with the modification of behavior is that it is only temporary. What you do not deal with will define you. What you ignore will imprison you. What you overlook will own you. These are the same individuals that we see caught up in scandals and questionable activities because they never took time to deal with the things that were trying to destroy them. Modification of behavior is proof of what you have not mastered. This is why Jericho is so important. Many of you reading this book can identify with what I just shared. You find yourself doing well for a little while but you are not really free. You have addictions, habits, hobbies, and secrets that own you. You desperately want to be free from them but they define you. It is time for you to come to Jericho. Too often we are fighting everyone and everything but ourselves. It is time to fight for your freedom and fight for your future. Stop making the battle about building something great and realize that the battle is about becoming who you were born to be. Most people are broken and defeated in life because they never win the battle to become. You cannot have true and lasting success until you win the battle to become. Jericho is the place where you come to the end of yourself. It is the place where you defeat the inner enemy. Jericho is where you land a deathblow to everything that stands between you and destiny. Jericho is the place of confrontation and the place where conquerors are birthed.

Are you not tired of fighting with yourself and losing? Are you ready to master the thing that has been manipulating your destiny? Then it is time to win the war in your mind. Many people think I am deep and profound now. However, for a long time, I was weak and powerless because I was losing the war in my soul. I had to learn how to bring every thought in my life into agreement with the truth of God's word. I had to learn how to superimpose truth over every lie that had tried to exalt itself above the knowledge of God. This was not an overnight process. This was years of doing the work to get whole in my soul and experience true freedom. I want to see liberated leaders leading around the world. I am tired of people trying to bring others into breakthroughs that they have not even experienced in their own lives. Stop trying to lead from your wounds and lead from a place of wholeness. I could not do what I do if I did not win the war in my soul and choose wholeness. I have had to encounter great spiritual warfare because God knew that my life would bring deliverance to the lives of many. The objective of spiritual warfare is to renew your mind to your true identity. Only then can you exercise your authority and walk in dominion. You cannot access the Kingdom without understanding your identity.

And Elijah said unto him, Tarry, I pray thee, here; for the LORD hath sent me to Jordan. And he said, As the LORD liveth, and as thy soul liveth, I will not leave thee. And they two went on. -2nd Kings 2: 6

I hope you have been paying attention to the different tests in this chapter. We now see Elijah giving Elisha another test. This time Elijah tests Elisha to see if he would follow him to Jordan. Now Jordan is the place of vision. Notice that you have to win the war for destiny before you can access the place of vision. If you are a leader working on your succession plan, never place a person in a position of leadership that has no vision. It is dangerous to have eyes that do not see. Yet I see so many people in positions of leadership today that have no vision. In fact, I have sat in meetings where I have watched visionless leaders become victims of those that they are supposed to be leading. Instead of providing insight and direction, I watched them sit back passively and let others dominate and determine the course. While I am not implying that there is anything wrong with delegation, the vision has to come from the top down. I could not imagine the CEO of Bank of America or Apple meeting with a board of advisors and sitting silently while the others communicate where they feel the company is going. You do not need a title of leadership to sit back passively and smile. Leaders see the future and then they empower organizations by pointing the way forward. If the leader does not know where he is going, then the followers are going to follow the leader right into a ditch. Elijah was taking Elisha to Jordan to see if he was a man of vision. Elijah wanted to see if he simply had eyes that look or eyes that see. Eyes that look are common. On the other hand, eyes that see are uncommon. Eyes that see produce what I call visionary leadership. Visionary leaders see the future, communicate the vision, develop the team and deploy them to see the vision become a reality. It is dangerous to place power in the hands of a person with no perception. After all, Elijah was the greatest prophetic voice of the era and he had to make sure that his legacy was in good hands. Do not bankrupt your legacy by empowering the blind to lead. Make sure that you are developing leaders of insight and vision.

Vision is the ability to imagine, plan and create the future through strategy and wisdom. Vision is not simply the ability to come up with concepts and ideas. Many people can come up with concepts and ideas. In addition, there are a lot of charismatic people in the world. Simply being charismatic does not make you a visionary leader. One thing I know about visionary leaders is that they have the ability to inspire, gather supporters and compel action. If you see a person constantly talking but never moving people to action then you need to take a good look at that person's leadership ability. Elijah was a prophet to the nations. Elijah had influence with kings, queens and even heads of nations. When Elijah spoke people listened because they respected him, they valued what he carried, and they recognized him as a man of God. In fact, Elijah was so influential that when he released the word of God Jezebel put a death threat on his life. In other words, she knew that when he spoke things happened. More importantly, Elijah stood in the counsel of God and had the ear of eternity. When Elijah spoke he literally shifted the spiritual destiny of nations. If you are going to succeed this kind of leader, then you have to be a person of vision and power. The reason we do not see the Elijah and Elisha model working in leadership today is because we have parasitical leaders that want what the mentor has. Furthermore, proteges want the heart of the leader and not the hand of the leader. Parasites just want to be promoted. However, proteges want to be processed. We have too many people that do not want to be processed to power and prominence in the world. This is why we have such a vacuum of leadership and that is what has created a leadership crisis.

Most people want to skip over Jericho and go right to Jordan. However, if you never win the war within you will never step into the vision and purpose that God has for you. You can try and use human ingenuity to bring the promise to pass in your life. However, when you use human ingenuity you birth Ishmael's.Essentially, Ishmael's are the things that blow up in your face and destroy you. You cannot fulfill your calling without God forging His nature and character in you. You cannot just overlook

Jericho and think you are going to step into Jordan. It is irresponsible to place vision in the hands of an immature leader. When you trust the immature with the vision you endorse illegal and illegitimate leadership. In other words, you guarantee the failure of cities, communities, organizations and nations. Why do I say this? You guarantee the death of your vision when you entrust it to individuals that have not been developed. Only leaders that have gone through seasons of forging are empowered to point the way forward. To place weight on a person that has not won the war in the soul will destroy your legacy and collapse your vision. If you have not heard anything that I have said up until this point, I want you to really grasp the magnitude of what I just shared with you. Stop setting future generations up for failure by promoting the gifted and not demanding a price for greatness. In all honesty, you do not respect what you carry when you cheapen the value of what it has taken a lifetime to build. You do not just want someone that can replace you. You want someone that can represent you. This is why not just anyone can be your successor. You only leave dynasties to those that possess your DNA.

And fifty men of the sons of the prophets went, and stood to view afar off: and they two stood by Jordan. And Elijah took his mantle, and wrapped it together, and smote the waters, and they were divided hither and thither, so that they two went over on dry ground.
-2nd Kings 2:7-8

It is a good thing that Elisha did not give up at Jericho. As we continue to excavate this pregnant prophetic text, we see so many keys for new and emerging leaders. Notice that the sons of the prophets stood to view from afar. In other words, they were willing to observe but never willing to follow. I believe this is so prophetic of what is still happening today. We have people that are observing leadership but never make the choice to follow. What most people do not understand is that observation does not exonerate you from the penalties of not fulfilling your prophetic destiny. Whether you choose to observe or engage, you will be held accountable for your assignment and what you did with the gift of your potential. Why study in the school of the prophets for years if you are not willing to follow the prophet Elijah into the next realm? Many are fascinated with the prophetic but they are not willing to go through the forging to stand as a powerful prophetic voice in the world. Students only get information but sons get impartations. It was essential that Elisha passed the test at Jordan. We see in this text that Elijah takes his mantle, wraps it together and smote the waters. Now that may not have prophetic significance to you but it has great significance to me. If you keep reading, it says that the waters were divided and they went over on dry ground. Why was it important that Elisha make it to Jordan? Yes, it was a miracle that he parted the waters but that is not what is most important here. After all, Elisha had been following the prophet for years and he already knew about miracles. The prophetic significance of this text is that they went over onto dry ground. So let me bring this concept home for you right now. After you have come through Gilgal and the cycle has been broken in your life. Then you have gone through Bethel and you have experienced the presence of God. Next, you go through Jericho and you win the war for destiny. Only then can you go to Jordan which is the place of vision. When your spiritual leader knows that the vision is solidified in you, then you can cross over into the next era of ministry. This is when Elisha went from prophetic development into prophetic destiny. This is the moment where Elisha crossed over from mentorship into ministry. This is the moment where Elisha moved from hand washer to next in line to carry on the prophetic ministry of Elijah. We have all heard the saying that when the student is ready the teacher will appear. Well, Elisha had passed all his tests and now God was promoting him into prophetic destiny. Commitment is the womb of crossing over. The sons of the prophets stood and watched from afar but Elisha stayed. Even when the senior prophet Elijah tried to shake him, Elisha was committed and he was not about to miss his moment. Elisha did not just come to Jordan and spectate. Elisha stepped over into his prophetic destiny. All this time Elisha had no clue that his commitment was qualifying him for his next. For every leader that is currently praying for their successor, I want you to discern between the observers and the committed. Elisha was released into his prophetic destiny because he was willing to follow the prophet into the next realm. Commitment will distinguish those that desire your position from those that carry your DNA. Have you identified those that are willing to follow?

Commitment is a word that has lost its meaning in the world today. In fact, it is difficult to find people that are willing to commit to anything. Almost every single day I hear from someone around the world wanting to be mentored, trained or developed by me. While I am always honored by the gesture, I know that very few will pass the test to ever be mentored by me. Why do I say that? I say that because most people are not really interested in mentorship. Most people want to pick my brain, hack success keys and go do their own thing. On the other hand, very few are willing to sit, unlearn everything that they think they know, learn from my journey and to submit their lives long enough to be developed for greatness. Nobody is interested in that because it is not a fast track to success. Nobody is interested in studying my life, my habits, my disciplines and the lessons that have shaped who I am today. Yet these same individuals think because they talk to me for an hour that they know who I am and can duplicate my success. What is the point that I am trying to make? We live in a celebrity fascinated culture where nobody wants to hear about discipline and commitment. Yet commitment is the very thing that will produce a world-class life, give you credibility and cause you to be on the cutting edge.

Commitment is not something that excites people. The reason that most people are not excited about commitment is because they have never committed to anything in life. We live in a culture and society that does not complete anything. We are constantly starting and stopping but we never accomplish anything. People look at my life and the things that I have been so fortunate to accomplish and they assume that many of these things happened overnight. However, I always tell people that I am a thirty year success story. In other words, I did not just wake up one day and become successful. It is the disciplines that I established day in and day out that has produced a life of success and prosperity. When others were playing I was praying. When others were wasting time I was working my plan. More importantly, when others were distracted I was consumed with developing the seed of my potential.

Now you see me stand on stages and deliver powerful keynotes. Also, you see me on television and featured in the pages of some of the biggest publications in the world. Then you see me connected to prominent and influential people. I did not get here because of wishful thinking or good intentions. I have created a world-class life because I was committed to greatness. Commitment is not based on the conditions in your life. Commitment is a conviction that will not let you settle for anything short of excellence in your life. My standards are what separate me from every other person on this planet. I have never seen development as a chore in my life. Instead, I have seen development as one of life's greatest pleasures. Commitment is making the decision to be dedicated to the fulfillment of your purpose and the maximization of your potential. Commitment is choosing mastery when everyone else is choosing mediocrity. Commitment is challenging yourself when others become complacent. Commitment is having the courage to pursue excellence when others prioritize easy. Commitment will not only distinguish you in the world but it will always give you access to dimensions that very few people ever reach. Commitment will shift you from common living into the realm of uncommon living. Are you committed to your destiny?

Honorable Living Exercises

1. What cycles need to be broken in your life?

2. How strong is your spiritual foundation?

3. What soul battles do you need to win?

4. Do you have eyes that look or eyes that see?

5. What is your vision?

Part 3:

Maximizing

"Maximizing your potential is going to the grave empty and knowing that you exhausted every seed of greatness within you."
-Jamelle Sanders

CHAPTER 7: THE POWER OF ASKING

"Asking is a powerful magnetic force attracting into your world success and prosperity or frustration and failure."
-Jamelle Sanders

And it came to pass, when they were gone over, that Elijah said unto Elisha, Ask what I shall do for thee, before I be taken away from thee. And Elisha said, I pray thee, let a double portion of thy spirit be upon me. -2nd Kings 2:9

As we delve deeper into this pregnant prophetic text, I want you to really pay attention to the remaining lessons in this book. What I am sharing with you will revolutionize your life and empower you to be a remarkable leader in your lifetime and generation. When I read this verse the thing that continues to jump out to me is the fact that it says when they were gone over. Remember that they just crossed over Jordan. Elijah simply extended an opportunity to Elisha. In all honesty, Elisha could have chosen to be an onlooker like the school of the prophets. However, Elisha was not content with just standing at the Jordan. Elisha made the decision to cross over. Many of you reading this book have been standing by and observing. However, you have to make the decision to cross over. While it is never easy to embrace new frontiers, you have to be fearless in your quest to seize your prophetic future. Elisha had given up everything and served Elijah faithfully for years. Elisha knew that what Elijah was carrying was essential to him fulfilling his calling. Empowered with courage Elisha made the decision to cross over. At this point, it was clear to Elijah that Elisha had passed the test of commitment. Despite all the distractions and attempts to break his focus Elisha remained fixed on his prophetic destiny. Most people are not willing to cross over because they have not fully committed to the thing that God has called and chosen them to do. Therefore, they are content with looking at what might be possible but never fulfilling the purpose and destiny that they were created for.

When Elisha made the decision to cross over, notice that Elijah then begins to have a conversation with him. Next level conversations do not begin in your life until you have the courage to cross over. There are conversations that you will never be invited into until you have the courage to cross over. What is calling you and beckoning you to the next realm in life? You know exactly what I am talking about. It is the uneasiness you feel on the inside. It is the discomfort and dissatisfaction with your life. You know you were made for more but you have settled for mediocrity. You have settled for the comfortable and convenient. You have done what was easy but you have been wired for excellence. Elisha passed the test of commitment and when he did he shattered the ceiling that stood between him and the next era of his life. When Elisha crossed over from Jordan, he not only shifted realms but he shifted the entire reality of his life. Jordan is the place of no return. It is the place where you learn to trust without borders, where you live beyond limits,where you build without boundaries.When you leave Jordan, you cross into the realm where faith is no longer just a law but a spiritual commodity by which all spiritual transactions, acquisitions, and negotiations occur. When you leave Jordan, you become alive to your true assignment and destiny. Crossing over connects you with the original conversation that you had with God in eternity past as it unfolds in the now.

Elijah asks Elisha to ask what he can do for him before he is taken away. I am trying to contain myself as I am writing this. I feel like running but I am forcing myself to sit and write so that you can get the revelation. Matthew 7:7 states "Ask, and it shall be given you; seek, and ye shall find; knock, and it shall be opened unto you." So many times we are cursing our lives and we do not even realize it. Oftentimes we are cursing the answers but failing to realize that we are asking the wrong questions. You do not need to curse the results. You need to reframe the questions that you are asking. The question is not what is wrong with my life. The real question is: what do I need to do to change my life? The question is not why is this happening to me. The real question is: how do I break this cycle in my life once and for all? You have to stop cursing the answer and examine whether or not you are asking the right questions. I have talked to so many people over the years that are living as products of their environments and prisoners to their circumstances. They have become so bound by the conditions in their lives that they have allowed their conditions to create the prophetic confessions and prophetic context of their lives. What they fail to understand is that questions frame language and language determines the answers that show up in your life. If you do not want it to show up in your moments, then you must never allow it to come out of your mouth. If you will dare to ask different questions, then you will get different answers. In addition, the quality of the questions you ask will determine the quality of the answers that you receive. You will never alter your life until you first adjust the questions that you are asking. Questions shape the quality of your life.

If you want to change a season in your life, then you first have to change the questions that you are asking. Questions unlock seasons in your life. In fact, when I have found myself in a very difficult place I often pull out my journal and sit in my thinking chair. I do not need to take any phone calls or respond to any emails. I do not need to have any conversations with anyone. All I need to do is take some time and think. I have discovered that when I sit still and take the time to think that I am able to dissect what had the appearance of a problem and discover solutions. You can think your way through anything. You can think your way around anything. You can think your way over anything. Most importantly, you can think your way out of anything. The problem is that most people never take the time to think. When you start asking the right questions, the right answers start showing up in your life. Right questions lead to right thinking which produces great breakthroughs in your life. I believe that asking is one of the most underutilized success strategies in the world. We spend too much time begging for what our brilliance can produce. You are so busy trying to rub shoulders that you never tap into real solutions. What you question you have the ability to challenge and ultimately change. Every solution is born out of a question. However, the absence of questions results in the absence of solutions. You have to stop being afraid to ask. Asking determines what you attract into your world. Your life is the actualization of what you have had the courage to ask for.

Asking is the womb of answers and we need leaders, trailblazers and history shapers that are not afraid to ask. Anyone will tell you that I am willing to ask hard questions. More importantly, I am willing to challenge conventional thinking. I am a revolutionary thinker because I have learned how to think outside of the box. In fact, my thinking has shattered paradigms, broken boundaries and birthed revolutions. I see too many leaders that are afraid to ask. When you are unwilling to ask you always limit yourself to average and mediocrity. On the other hand, when you dare to ask you access realms of excellence and mastery. All advancements and innovations are born out of those that had the courage to ask and to act. I wonder how many of you are going to have the audacity to start asking bold questions and advancing humanity. What you are not willing to ask for you will never attract into your world. You can create a million vision boards and write out a ton of affirmations. However, at some point, you must have the courage to speak up and ask the right questions if you want to alter the trajectory of your life. When we ask the wrong questions, we disempower our lives and we live on repeat. On the other hand, when we ask the right questions we empower our lives, reverse cycles and ultimately reframe our worlds. From science to education, we have been taught all our lives to question and challenge things. Yet so many people in the world today are afraid to ask anything. We often ask the obvious and we get disappointed. Very few ask distinct questions and access new discoveries and solutions. The solutions you seek exist in another realm. However, you have to upgrade your mind to think differently, think non traditionally, think radically, think intergenerationally, think strategically, think tactically and think originally.

Elijah poses the question to Elisha to ask what he can do for him before he is taken. Notice that commitment was the catalyst to crossing over and unlocking the next season of his destiny. More importantly, crossing over opens the conversation to ask for what he wants. This brings me all the way back to the beginning of this book. This text about asking what he wants is a prophetic fulfillment of a prophetic process that had been initiated in Elisha's life years ago. What am I saying? His commitment is what gave him access to ask. We have too many people asking for what they have not been willing to invest and serve for. Elisha had qualified to ask because he had proven his commitment and he had passed the test. I also want you to pay attention to the fact that Elijah did not ask Elisha the question until they were away from the school of the prophets. In other words, sometimes your associations are robbing you of the access and opportunity to ask for what you want. Elijah shows us another very important lesson in succession planning and strategy. Never allow the parasites access into the portion that belongs to the proteges. Two important things have to happen in order to unlock a season of asking in your life. First of all, you have to be processed in order to embrace a season of asking. Processed means that you have to be developed to access certain dimensions. Secondly, you have to be proven to unlock a season of asking in your life. Process is about development but being proven is about staying power. In essence, being proven is being built to last and this is something missing in the lives of many that call themselves leaders today.

Questions are the womb of quantum leaps. As someone that has had the pleasure of working with leaders around the world, anybody that has ever worked with me will tell you that I never go into a session without questions. In fact, if you have read my books you will discover that every book is filled with questions. Why is that? Questions are what changed my life. It was the discovery that my life was not working that prompted me to ask questions. However, I did not just ask any questions. I started asking the questions that would lead me to the answers that I had been looking for my entire life. Questions hold the power to unlock and upgrade you. Asking is a simple spiritual law that holds the power to produce massive shifts and quantum leaps in your life. Asking is the womb of acceleration. Asking is a Kingdom technology that unlocks prophetic destiny. Often we are analyzing when what we really need is the audacity to ask. One answer from eternity can end a lifetime of questions. I want to unpackage that for a moment. Elisha knew all his life that he was destined for more. It was the reason he could not be content plowing with the twelve yoke of oxen. This is the same reason that he could not be satisfied taking over the family business. Elisha knew that he was made for so much more. He could not articulate it but he had enough prophetic acumen and perceptivity to realize that this is not it. Well, let me announce to you that what Elisha was discerning was destiny. While he did not have all the pieces of his prophetic puzzle, Elisha had perception and he had a prophetic prompting that set him on a path to prophetic destiny. Awareness brought alignment to his life and divinely orchestrated a moment of asking. This awareness caused Elisha to abandon everything he had ever known to embrace a destiny not yet born to time. Elisha did not need information, validation or confirmation. Elisha had a word from God and that was all he needed. Do you have a word from God? Are you synchronized and syncopated with heaven's rhythm? Are you in step with earth or are you in step with eternity? I am sure some of you are wondering how to even answer this. However, you do not have to look really far to answer these questions. All you have to do is look at your life and it will tell you if you are in the correct prophetic longitudes and latitudes. There is prosperity that comes with being in the right prophetic zip code. On the other hand, there are consequences when we get out of the right prophetic coordinates. Obedience keeps you in sync with God's timing. Disobedience will cost you seasons and interrupt your destiny. Your cycles are a reflection of what you have come into covenant with. Ultimately, what you come into covenant with sets the course of your destiny.

Asking demands maturity and development. Many people are observing others walking into prophetic destiny. However, a lack of obedience prohibits them from inheriting the promise. If you want to know how mature you are, then look at the nature of your asking. Bold asking is only produced through brokenness. You cannot ask godly desires without a great death. Much of the asking I see today is for personal benefit and not the building of the Kingdom of God. A person that has not been crushed is too conceited to surrender to the cause of Christ. Agendas die when you take on your Kingdom assignment. Ambition has no place in the advancement of the Kingdom of God. Ego has no relevance when eternity becomes your priority. Pride must be destroyed to take your place in the Kingdom. When the immature ask, the result is a life that is led and governed by the nature of the soul. Conversely, when the mature ask they are empowered to follow their northstar and manifest heaven on earth. In other words, asking is not a wish list but a will shift. The will of man plays a vital role in the unfolding of God's plan for humanity. Without the surrendering of your will, you will never be entrusted with significant work in the Kingdom. Many are called but few ever qualify. In order to qualify, you have to graduate from the pull of success and notoriety to the privilege of service. You grow into access and you graduate into asking. Then when you get your opportunity to ask you will appreciate it.

Asking is the catalyst to advancement. Every major ascension and awakening in your life is the result of asking. In life, you do not get what you aspire to have. You do not get what you have the ambition for. No, you get in life exactly what you have the courage to ask for. If you have read my books, then you know I talk about how shy, timid and unsure of myself I was. As I started to do the work, I realized my value, discerned my worth and awakened to my significance. My relationship constellation started to change. I stopped looking for quantity in relationships and started demanding quality. In the process, I attracted into my life powerful and influential people. Many of these individuals I now consider friends, mentors and advisors. I do not come into their presence with small talk and useless contributions. Instead, I enter their presence with questions. I understand that I have an incredible opportunity to listen to wisdom, gather insights and learn truths that have the power to accelerate my learning curve and my success. Why is this so important? Elijah simply extended an invitation to the young emerging prophet Elisha. Elijah did not come with big gimmicks or promises for Elisha. No, Elijah simply presented Elisha with the opportunity to invest the gift of time to one day manifest the potential and possibilities that were dormant within him not yet born to time. In essence, a simple invitation changed the course of Elisha's destiny forever. It gave him the opportunity to learn, study, mature, develop and serve the life of one of the greatest prophets to ever live. All of this set Elisha up for the opportunity to cross over the Jordan. Elisha moved beyond prophetic dimensions and accessed prophetic realms. When he stepped into the prophetic realm, Elisha exposed him to a new Kingdom technology. In fact, I often say that Elijah gave sound to the prophetic sensing that Elisha had been feeling all his life. Elisha followed Elijah without the senior prophet ever telling him why he was following him. Elisha had no guarantee of his prophetic future but he had a prophetic prompting. That prompting positioned him for a moment of asking for what he knew was possible his entire life. I wonder what is really possible for you that you have not had the courage to ask for. When you ascend into the next realm, know that heaven will always extend an opportunity to ask. By the time you grow into access and graduate into asking, you will be mature enough to discern the significance of that moment in your life. Asking moves you out of the realm of facts and information and into the realm of truth and revelation. God matures the man, develops his faith and shapes him for a moment of bold asking. Your asking is always in proportion to your faith. Faith is a currency and patience is a virtue. These power twins are how you inherit the promises of God. Asking unlocks the realm of Kingdom exchanges. Everything in the Kingdom of God is paid for by faith.

Honorable Living Exercises

1. Are you ready to cross over into the next season of your life?

2. Are you cursing your life by asking the wrong questions?

3. How will you reframe your question and shift your season?

4. What answers are you tapping into?

5. When will you develop the courage to ask for what you want?

6. Have you cultivated the faith to ask big and access the realm of limitless possibilities and opportunities?

Chapter 8: Discerning Moments of Opportunity

"Kingdom success and Kingdom greatness
will demand that you cultivate the discipline
of seizing moments of opportunity."
-Jamelle Sanders

And it came to pass, when they were gone over, that
Elijah said unto Elisha, Ask what I shall do for thee,
before I be taken away from thee. And Elisha said, I
pray thee, let a double portion of thy spirit be upon
me.

And he said, Thou hast asked a hard thing:
nevertheless, if thou see me when I am taken from
thee, it shall be so unto thee; but if not, it shall not be
so.

And it came to pass, as they still went on, and talked,
that, behold, there appeared a chariot of fire, and
horses of fire, and parted them both asunder; and
Elijah went up by a whirlwind into heaven.

2nd Kings 2:9-11

If you were to ask me for a key to success and
prosperity, I would probably mention things like
mindset, intention, discipline, identity, consistency,
and other factors. However, one of the greatest keys

to success and prosperity in my life has been the ability to perceive and seize moments of opportunity in my life. In fact, I can look back over the last thirty-plus years and identify specific times where I was able to perceive moments of opportunity and propel my life forward. One of the skills that I see missing in the lives of so many people in the world today is the skill of discernment. Discernment is the ability to recognize what is not obvious to the naked eye. In fact, I often say that discernment is the ability to see the invisible and seize the impossible. This skill set has empowered me to be a visionary and innovative leader. In other words, discernment has given me an edge and helped me to break barriers and push boundaries. Elisha is someone that mastered the art of discerning moments of opportunity. We can go back to the initial meeting between Elijah and Elisha in the field. It was discernment that caused Elisha to recognize a moment of opportunity, recklessly abandon everything that was familiar to him, and to pursue a reality not yet born to time. When I look around the world today, it is difficult to identify Elisha's. Everyone wants to be promoted to the next level but nobody perceives the key moments and inflection points that position you to seize new possibilities and opportunities for your life. You need to develop this skill of discernment or you will never step into your prophetic destiny. You will always be standing on the outside looking in but never seizing opportunities in your life. Discernment is a discipline that has to be developed and it takes time. Most people have to be told what to do but when you have discernment you will know exactly what to do. Knowledge without discernment results in confusion. On the other hand, knowledge coupled with discernment produces clarity. Discernment unlocks new dimensions in your life.

As we discovered in the last chapter, Elisha's willingness to follow Elijah even without the guarantee of a reward is remarkable. The school of the prophets observed Elijah and Elisha but they never had the courage to follow. They were content with just watching from a distance. However, Elisha's courage to follow empowered him to cross over into a new realm of possibilities and opportunities. It was after they crossed over that the invitation was extended to Elisha to ask for what he wanted. In other words, his willingness to follow Elijah forward was a prophetic catalyst into his future. His ability to discern a moment of opportunity was a doorway into his prophetic destiny. We find Elisha presented with an incredible opportunity to ask for what he wanted. If you recall, in the last chapter I talked about how Elisha was never given the opportunity to ask until he had crossed over into a place of vision. In other words, some things will never be possessed in your life without perception. Eyes that look are common but eyes that can see are rare. I am not talking about having mere sight. I am talking about having prophetic acumen and perceptivity. I am talking about having the ability to see into another realm and create a new reality. I am talking about having insight. Insight makes the invisible tangible and the impossible inevitable. This is not a realm reserved for a select few. This is a realm that you have to be trained to access. According to Hebrews 5:4 "But strong meat belongeth to them that are of full age, even those who by reason of use have their senses exercised to discern both good and evil." In essence, it takes maturity, growth, and development to have insight. Your spiritual senses have to be exercised to discern moments of opportunity and possibility in your life. Elisha had served Elijah faithfully for years. While some will consider his job menial, the thing that they do not understand is that God was using all of this to mold Elisha for a greater mission. In the process of pouring water on the hands of Elijah for years, God was building in Elisha character, consistency, humility, a servant heart, discipline, acumen, and the perceptivity to pierce into another realm. Ultimately, in his serving God was empowering Elisha to live a supernatural life. The school of the prophets only observed but Elisha was given access to the life and ministry of Elijah. Observing keeps you at a distance. On the other hand, following allows you access to see up close and personal the inner workings of the life and ministry of

Elijah. Observation only gives you knowledge but being willing to follow gives you intimacy. The thing that I love about intimacy is that it is the catalyst to all transformation in your life. Many people are trying to perceive moments of opportunity when they are not even positioned to perceive moments of opportunity in their lives. You will never receive an impartation without insight. Insight empowers you to be in proper alignment. When you are in proper alignment you are given access to mantles and anointings. Alignment brings both acumen and acuity. The school of the prophets followed from a distance and all that produced was admiration in their lives. However, Elisha stayed close and he was granted access to the anointing of one of the greatest prophets to ever live. Insight does not come without connection. Over the years, I have discovered that destiny connections cannot be formed without clarity. Clarity will empower you to find your tribe and unlock the treasures that God has placed on the inside of you. Without clarity you will always be connecting out of desperation and never out of destiny. Desperation only attracts dysfunctional relationships into your life. On the other hand, discernment will empower you to attract destiny relationships into your life that will aid your mission. Discernment will empower you to distinguish between the leeches and the loyal in your life.

When Elisha was presented with his moment of opportunity he perceived it and he was prepared for it. Elisha responds by saying let a double portion of your spirit be upon me. In the previous chapter, I talked about coming into the presence of greatness with the right questions. You never want to waste the time of great people. You should ask deep questions. Furthermore, you should ask questions that have the power to unlock your destiny. Many people from around the world will read this book and I hope you will highlight this section in particular. Beggars never prosper and beggars never reach their full potential. Begging is for those that do not understand their covenant or how to exercise their rights. Elisha was not a beggar. Elisha was someone that perceived the significance of a moment in his life. Elisha had been pondering this thought in his mind for a long time. While he was not sure when the moment would come, Elisha understood the power of asking. More importantly, Elisha understood that asking had the power to awaken him to his assignment and activate his prophetic destiny. Elisha took his time and served faithfully for years. Elisha served without fame or fanfare. Elisha served without the need for recognition or applause. Elisha knew that Elijah was carrying something that had the power to change his life. So Elisha waited patiently for his moment to come. When Elisha perceived that the time was right, the womb of the spirit was pregnant, and conditions were favorable, Elisha dared to ask a bold question. Bold questions require bold faith. What Elisha was asking for was going to require great faith and great courage. In essence, Elisha did not just want to be a student of the prophetic. Elisha wanted to be a protege of the prophetic. Elisha wanted the DNA of the life and ministry of Elijah to be identifiable and imprinted on him. Elisha wanted to be the seal of the prophetic ministry of Elijah and not just a student. Elisha wanted an impartation that would empower him to impact nations and generations. Elisha was perceptive and prepared to seize a key moment of opportunity in his life. What you cannot perceive you will never possess. Destiny is aborted by those that lack the discernment to make key shifts and turns.

How did Elisha know what to ask for? Elisha understood the dynamics of this Kingdom relationship. Elisha understood that he was not just sent to Elijah to serve and pour water on his hands. From the very beginning, Elisha knew that Elijah was carrying something that he needed. Furthermore, Elisha understood that the key to unlocking his prophetic destiny was locked up in Elijah. I will take it a step further and say that the pieces of his prophetic destiny could not come together without Elijah. Elijah was the key to Elisha unlocking what he was born for. Elijah was the combination to the vault that would unlock the treasures of the Kingdom that had been buried deep in Elisha awaiting activation and expression. Some relationships come into your life for a moment. Other relationships come into your life for a season. However, some relationships come into your life for destiny. Your ability to perceive properly the relationships in your life will determine your peace, your prosperity, your promotion, and your progression. When you extend expired relationships you endanger your future. Trying to hold on to relationships that you have outgrown will only oppose your destiny. Some relationships come into your life to undermine you. Other relationships show up in your life to upgrade you. Most importantly, destiny relationships show up in your life to unlock you. If you can discern the relationships that are sent into your life to unlock you, then you can unleash your greatest potential and become unstoppable. Elisha discerned a destiny relationship in his life and he did not allow anything to disrupt that relationship. No battle had the ability to break the bond between Elijah and Elisha. Never fight for relationships that cater to your dysfunctions. Make the decision to fight for destiny relationships in your life. Dysfunctional relationships feed your weaknesses but destiny relationships empower your wholeness. Relationships determine the realm that you live from. Make sure that your relationship constellation is not restricting your capacity for greatness.

In a lifetime, most people never discover destiny relationships. Most people cling to the familiar because they lack the courage to pursue the future. In reality, most people just want to be connected to something even if it has no significance. Why? Any association is better than being alone. Trust me I have been there and I have written extensively about this topic. What I have discovered is that wrong relationships cost you time, opportunities, progress, freedom and peace. Any relationship that does not move me in the direction of my destiny is a relationship that does not belong in my life. I refuse to cling to anything that is going to cripple my life. I learned that some people I do not need and they are simply no good for my life. It is not even that they are terrible people or toxic relationships. I simply discovered that our lives were headed in totally opposite directions. I cannot reroute the course of my destiny just for the sake of preserving a relationship that has no value in my life. You have to come to a point where you get tired of pulling dead weight. Some people only bring your life down. They do not benefit you in any way and they do not make your life better. At some point, you have to dare to say goodbye to what is familiar and say hello to your future. You deserve to embrace the destiny that God has for your life. Elisha realized that he could settle for the safety of community or pursue the significance of a destiny connection. Elisha's willingness to burn the past was the seed that birthed him into his prophetic destiny. He realized that the cost of staying behind would produce spiritual barrenness in his life. When more is calling you it takes maturity to have the courage to pursue it.

Events shape us and engineer moments of significance in our lives. Elisha did not realize that what he was willing to say no to in another season was setting him up for saying yes to his season of destiny. It does not cost much to remain a student. However, it will cost you everything to become a protege. What you are willing to walk away from will determine what you are able to ask for in another season. Elisha could ask extravagantly because he had given God everything. God had Elisha's time, talent and treasures. You will never seize a moment without service. Too many people are trying to step onto platforms that they have not been processed to stand on. Serving is important because that is how God molds us to step into our moment. Elisha had passed the test and promotion was in his future. As the prophetic protege of Elijah, Elisha perceived a moment of opportunity and God partnered with him in that moment. God does not partner with everyone. However, God will partner with those that have pure hearts and Kingdom priorities. Elisha was able to perceive a moment of opportunity because he had been trained and developed for it. Proclamation without preparation will only produce frustration. Proclamation coupled with preparation will produce fruitfulness. In other words, God will always prove you before he promotes you. Elisha had won the war for destiny and now promotion was happening in his life. Elisha was able to interpret moments correctly because he possessed prophetic insight. When you possess insight you have access to the unseen realm and tap into that which is not yet born to time. Elisha was able to master moments because he was mature and developed.

No moment can be seized and no season can be captured in your life without maturity. The difference in seasons is maturity. The difference in relationships is maturity. Your maturity will determine what you manifest in your life. You cannot simply get excited about the potential of a moment if you have not been processed for that moment. Nobody else had the legal right to ask Elijah to be the successor but Elisha. Why do I say this? Elisha sowed his life in service to Elijah. Only a mature person would be willing to submit their entire life to the service of another man's vision. Never consider a succession plan where sacrifice has not been a pillar in the life of the person taking on the new role of leadership. Seizing moments has everything to do with spiritual maturity. Discernment involves the ability to judge or distinguish accurately. In other words, seizing moments is having the ability to distinguish the significance of a moment in your life. It is the ability to separate the urgent from the important, the divine from distractions, and the time sensitive from the trivial. This is a skill set that requires patience, process, perception and prophetic acumen to master. Honestly, if more people knew the power of moments then they would never waste another moment of their lives. If opportunity demands preparation, then we can take it a step further and say that success is the product of preparation, perception and opportunity colliding. Therefore, seizing moments demands that we live with an urgency and intentionality because life is fleeting and every moment is precious. Moments cannot be recaptured and demand recognition. Failure to recognize moments will result in a lifetime of regret. Seizing moments is understanding times and seasons and being able to recognize the significance of moments in your life. Elisha recognized that a season had ended and that time had shifted in his life. More importantly, Elisha realized the brevity of the time he had left with Elijah. In that moment, Elisha did what any mature person would do. Elisha discerned the significance of the time and used it as an opportunity to change his season. With courage, Elisha dared to ask an uncommon question and unlocked an uncommon season in his life. Elisha had waited a lifetime for this moment and he was not going to miss it. Elisha had to be mature enough to realize that the departure of his mentor was the doorway into a new mantle in his life. While Elijah was being taken away from Elisha, this significant moment was the transfer of power to the next generation. Transfers of power are threatened where there is no perception.

Maturity defines the motion of your life. So many people are drawn to power and success. However, they do not understand that success is a garment that you have to grow into. You cannot just put on success. No, you have to be processed to success. The only way you will ever grow into the garment of success is through development. Maturity is produced when the pain of growth becomes more important than the pleasure of gratification. The school of the prophets enjoyed the pleasure of gratification. They liked being distanced from Elijah because it did not require development. More importantly, no demands will be made on you as long as you follow from a distance. So it was gratifying for them to learn about and observe the life of Elijah. However, they had no interest in serving and submitting their lives to the leadership of Elijah for mentorship. They were only interested in the display of gifts and not the development of their gifts. Over the last three decades, I have learned that without the right mentorship in your life you will never discover your gift and you will never develop your gift. In other words, there are things in you that will never be expressed without the right mentors and advisors in your life. The school of the prophets had prophetic potential but Elisha was willing to go through a prophetic process. Maturity is the key to mounting great platforms and maintaining great platforms. Maturity is the reason that so many people are never able to discern moments of opportunity in their lives. Without maturity, you will waste seasons, squander moments and bury the seed of your potential. When we live without maturity we lack wisdom, fail to possess insight, live without clarity, and repeat cycles because we cannot recognize the importance of times and seasons in our lives. Moments that are not seized are moments that you let slip away from you. To allow moments to slip away is to dishonor the seed of your potential.

You will never seize moments as long as you are fascinated with your gifts. Anybody can have a gift. However, the ability to govern your gift is what will define your greatness. I look around the world today and I see many gifted people. At the same time, I look around the world and I do not see nearly as many great people. Why is that? Gifts without growth become forgettable. In contrast, when we combine gifts and growth in our lives we become unforgettable. Recognition in the world will be the product of your respect for your gift. The school of the prophets did not respect their gifts. How do I know that? Any person that respects their gifts will refine their gifts. Do not tell me that you respect your gifts and you are not constantly working to refine your gifts. Most people are just happy with having a gift. Very few people truly honor their gifts. Elisha was not content to just have a gift but he was committed to honoring his gift. Your gifts cannot be refined without development. Refinement empowers you to recognize and seize moments of opportunity in your life. The school of the prophets does not teach you how to refine your gift or recognize moments of opportunity in your life. The school of the prophets only provides knowledge. Refinement provides Kingdom insights. We live in a generation that loves knowledge but lacks insight. Knowledge is limited but insight gives you access to new realms. Refinement is the key to a regret-free life. Refinement is the key to recognition and reclamation of everything that belongs to you. Refinement is the catalyst by which you realize your full potential and release the greatness within you. Some things you do not learn in the classroom. Some things can only be learned in the crucibles of life. God will never serve you to the world until you are refined. There are many that will never qualify because they chose to overlook the prophetic process. You learn much more in the field than you learn in the classroom. Elisha not only had textbook knowledge but he had experienced and encountered prophetic ministry. More importantly, Elisha had been trained and developed because he did not just stop at observation and education. Elisha dared to pursue mentorship and prophetic development. His willingness to endure the pain of growth is what propelled greatness in his life. Elisha could perceive what others could not because he had paid a price that others were not willing to pay. Opportunities are never seized standing on the outside looking in. Opportunities are seized by those with the courage and passion to perceive and pursue. Elisha's pursuit became a portal into his prophetic future. Never settle for simply being in the company of greatness. Always stretch your capacity to manifest the greatness that is within you!

Honorable Living Exercises

1. Do you have discernment?

2. Is your perception robbing you of a new season in your life?

3. Are you operating from a place of clarity?

4. Are you perceptive enough to know what to ask for?

5. Do you have momentary, seasonal or destiny relationships in your life?

6. Have you matured to step into your moment?

7. Will you seize moments of opportunity in your life?

CHAPTER 9: HONOR

"Honor is not just a law but a constitution that governs every relationship on this planet."
-Jamelle Sanders

And it came to pass, when they were gone over, that Elijah said unto Elisha, Ask what I shall do for thee, before I be taken away from thee. And Elisha said, I pray thee, let a double portion of thy spirit be upon me.

And he said, Thou hast asked a hard thing: *nevertheless*, if thou see me *when I am* taken from thee, it shall be so unto thee; but if not, it shall not be *so*.

And it came to pass, as they still went on, and talked, that, behold, *there appeared* a chariot of fire, and horses of fire, and parted them both asunder; and Elijah went up by a whirlwind into heaven.

2nd King 2:9-11

As we approach the end of this book, I hope that you are really comprehending these concepts and principles. You may have to read this book several times before it really becomes clear to you exactly what I am talking about. I believe that honor is not just a law that governs greatness. No, I believe that honor is a constitution that governs every relationship on this planet. Years ago, I found myself continually attracting toxic relationships into my life. I found myself surrounded by treacherous, conniving, vindictive, opportunistic and artificial people. It was not making sense to me why I was attracting these relationships into my life. Then one day I had an epiphany and it changed the course of my life forever. I realized that my assessment of myself will always determine the associations that I attract into my life. In other words, my relationship constellation is simply a realization of the self-concept that I hold about myself. My associations reveal to me what I have assessed my worth and value as a human being to be. That day I sat down and made an intentional decision to renegotiate the terms of every relationship in my life. If you have followed my work over the years, then you have heard me speak many times about renegotiating the terms of the relationships in your life. Over the years, I have scanned audiences to see people cheering and applauding but not comprehending and applying the wisdom that I was sharing with them. As long as your assessment of yourself is low, you will continue to attract dysfunctional destiny-aborting relationships in your life. However, the moment you awaken to your true value and significance, every leech and every snake will have no choice but to vacate the premises of your life and abide by the terms of your contractual agreement. This powerful principle will shift your life forever! Redefining the terms of the relationships in your life is not a task that you can relegate to another human being. You alone are responsible for defining and negotiating the terms of every relationship in your life.

I am sure that some of you are wondering what exactly does this have to do with honor or Elijah and Elisha. On the contrary, what we fail to understand is that honor is the pillar of strong, healthy, authentic relationships. For years, I allowed people to use, abuse and trample on me because that is all I felt I was worth. Later, I came to the discovery that not one of those relationships truly honored me. You depreciate your value every single time you tolerate dishonorable relationships in your life.Currently, I am very pleased with the relationship constellation in my life. Instead of being desperate for relationships, I discern those that God has divinely assigned to me. In addition, I make people qualify for my time, I do not give everyone access to my life, and I do not allow people to speak to me in a condescending manner. I have learned how to love myself unconditionally. More importantly, I have learned that the relationships in my life are a reflection of the respect that I have for myself and the calling on my life. As someone that has had the pleasure of speaking with leaders from all around the world, we do not have nearly as many organizational problems as we think. The real challenge that I see around the world is a lack of honor. Everyone is competing for first place and to be the center of attention. As for me, I am more interested in showing up in rooms where I can feel honor. We cannot heal the great divide among leaders in the world until we first learn how to honor one another. One day I was observing what appeared to be a persistent challenge among a group of leaders. Then, I had a thought that I immediately wrote down and I share it with people everywhere I go. How do we move humanity forward? What is the key to creating effective succession plans? How do we correctly transfer power from generation to generation? You can only marry generations through honor. Where there is dishonor you will always find division and divisiveness. As a leader that has had to navigate working with different generations, I have seen firsthand the impact of people trying to work together that have no honor for one another. We have organizations filled with people that tolerate each other but do not trust or honor one another. I have sat in rooms and seen people that just want to get their point across but have no desire to connect and understand different perspectives. Also, I know what it feels like to be the young person in the room that is looked over, discounted and ultimately dismissed as having nothing relevant or meaningful to contribute to the conversation. In my younger years, I allowed this to bother me and even shut me down from operating in my gifts. Conversely, as I matured I realized that I am mantled to push boundaries and break barriers. I am anointed to sit at the table and to challenge old mindsets, systems and protocols. As I recognized my power, I became respected at various tables and with humility showed generations how to work together to propel radical change and to ultimately move humanity forward. In essence, I have discovered that if we cannot work together then we can never effectively build anything great together.

While some people see the story of Elijah and Elisha as just another bible story, I see this as a Kingdom expression of what honor looks like. You find Elisha a young promising business man that comes from a wealthy family. Elisha is next in line to run the empire and the community has already labeled Elisha as the successor. Nobody in the community could perceive that what they had destined Elisha for was causing a spiritual death in his life. Elisha was wrestling with the need to please everyone around him. Inside Elisha was spiritually dying and spiritually deprived. Elisha knew that he had been destined for more but his culture wanted to constrict him to a small place. Elisha was carrying something that was bigger than the region that birthed him. Elisha was pregnant with something that his culture and community did not have the capacity to contain or conceive. Elisha could have done the noble thing of trying to please everybody. However, the cost to his spiritual destiny would have been detrimental. Elisha could have innovated and helped take the family business to the next level. After all, he would have won all kinds of awards and been celebrated in the community for his brilliant mind. Elisha could have kept plowing in the field but he would have never been able to partner with his prophetic destiny. What would cause a man to leave so much opportunity behind to embrace a reality unknown to time? I can tell you unequivocally that it was destiny. Elisha abandons everything to follow a man that did not even call him by name. Elisha follows a man that simply cast his mantle on him. This powerful prophetic text is so pregnant. While we see no words being spoken, what happened in that moment would forever shape the course of Elisha's destiny forever. When the mantle was cast on his shoulders, for the first time in his life Elisha felt his baby leap. What am I talking about? As a prophetic intercessor, Elisha had been picking up prophetic promptings and stirrings. Elisha knew that something was about to happen. Elisha had a sensing that God was challenging him to follow him into the great unknown. When Elijah cast that mantle on Elisha, he felt alive and his spirit was set on fire. Elisha knew that the pain of departing the familiar could not compare to the divine future that was beckoning him. Elisha had gotten a glimpse of his prophetic future and courageously said goodbye to his history and hello to his destiny. Elisha did not have all the details or the pieces but he had the ability to recognize that more was available to him and that God was presenting him with the opportunity to partner with the mission he was made for. What appeared to be an interruption became a divine invitation to embrace his prophetic destiny. What you currently see as a setback could be a divine setup for a season of greatness and significance in your life. Refuse to be blinded by the familiar and make a quality decision that you will not allow anything to rob you of your prophetic future.

Honor is a word that you do not hear talked about very much today. In fact, I do not hear the word used very much at all. In an individualistic society and egotistical culture, honor is a word that invokes bewildered looks and disgusted expressions. Yet, honor has been the key to my promotion, progression and my prosperity. The only reason God has allowed me to ascend into high places of influence and power is because I understand the law of honor. If you want to do great things in your lifetime, then you need to master the law of honor. If you want to go higher in leadership and power, then you need to master a life of humility. I have never seen so much pride and arrogance in the world. What I know from years of experience is that a person that is filled with pride and arrogance has not been broken. However, if you keep living long enough you will arrive at a place of brokenness in your life. In fact, I often say if God cannot break you then life will certainly teach you a masterful lesson in brokenness. I see people today competing for positions, fighting for power and feeling entitled to lead. However, what I do not see enough of is servant leaders that lead with pure hearts and no personal agendas. Everyone wants to rise to the top but nobody wants to serve. Nobody wants to be processed to a position of power and influence in the world. Do you really want to lead? Then you need to choose the path of the lowly. What do I mean by this? Elisha went from being next in line to run an empire to silent years of pouring water on the hands of the prophet Elijah. You talk about a downgrade in lifestyle. I am sure that to the outside world it made no logical sense why Elisha would recklessly abandon everything only to end up washing the hands of Elijah. However, what the outside world could not understand is that silent years are always pregnant with significance. During the silent years God was teaching Elisha a master class in obedience and submission to authority. When you say the word submission to most people, you may as well have made an explicit statement or remark. In all honesty, most people see submission as a form of weakness and powerlessness. On the other hand, I see submission as a form of strength and power in the life of an effective leader. What you have to understand is that all power that has no governance is counterfeit. More importantly, power without governance will only produce corrupt leadership. The corrosion of systems and institutions is always the result of corrupt leadership. Matthew 8: 9 states "For I am a man under authority, having soldiers under me: and I say to this *man*, Go, and he goeth; and to another, Come, and he cometh; and to my servant, Do this, and he doeth *it*." In other words, effective leaders understand that the legitimacy of power demands that one be both in authority and under authority. In essence, there is no true ascension without accountability. Furthermore, without accountability no leader has true authority. Elisha understood that the key to accessing his prophetic destiny was understanding this principle of submission and honor. Elisha recognized that if he wanted to fulfill his prophetic destiny then he first had to be a leader that was under the authority of a greater leader. We live in the era of the bastard. The bastard wants to shine but violently opposes any form of submission. Elisha realized that all success is born out of submission. What do I mean by this? Elisha understood that honor is the seed for access and ascension. This fledgling prophetic voice understood that growing up was the key to going up. In other words, it is not enough to recognize the greatness on another person's life. No, you must take it a step further and respect the greatness that is on another person's life. What you do not respect you will always repel from your life. What you respect you are entitled to receive from. Elisha recognized the anointing on Elijah's life and he made the decision to serve that anointing. You will never be mantled with an anointing that you have not served.

While some have abused power and perpetuated false truths about submission and honor of leadership, I want to take a moment and say that honor is the only authentic way to transfer power and to ensure succession of leadership for generations to come. As I have sat with emerging leaders over the years, I have listened as they have shared their trepidations about submitting to senior leadership. I have heard the horror stories of abuse, manipulation and coercion over the years. These experiences have traumatized many and caused them to rebel against anything that resembles submission to authority. On the other hand, I know firsthand that with prophetic acumen and perceptivity God will send you to safehouses where apostolic and prophetic leadership can train, equip, empower and develop you to fulfill your prophetic destiny. Many people around the world recognize me as a thought leader and admire the work that I do around the world. However, what they fail to understand is that my understanding of the law of honor is what has promoted me to where I am today. My willingness to invite correction, pursue accountability and have spiritual leaders that hold me to high moral standards of personal integrity is the reason I am able to write this book today. I am not telling you something I looked up online or grabbed out of a book. I am telling you that I am doing things today that I never imagined I would do. I am operating in capacities that I did not even know that I had. How did I get here? I allowed leaders to become hands-on in my personal growth and development. While I have had to endure seasons of correction and calibration, all of it has made me the man that I am today. I never knew that I had been gifted with the ability to communicate. Nor did I ever imagine I would write books, serve in high leadership capacities and be highly involved in training and developing other leaders. I am literally doing things that I never in a million years saw myself doing. Today, I am operating in gifts and talents that I never knew were inside of me until I allowed senior leaders to pull these giftings out of me. You may be talented on your own. However, you will never be refined without great leaders and mentors in your life. You have so much to contribute to the world but you have to be developed to unleash your true capacity for greatness. Gifts without growth and development produce ego. Conversely, gifts coupled with growth and development produce excellence and make you an exceptional leader. I am not negating the fact that you have the potential to be great. However, what I am saying is that the grave is filled with potential that died and never contributed anything to humanity. Everybody has potential but very few people know how to convert that potential into greatness. No person succeeds alone. Honor is the foundation for success and prosperity in your life. There is a prophetic grid for your life. There is a spot that God has assigned you to where you will awaken to the significance within you. It has been in you all your life but it is only unlocked through the right leaders and mentors. Find your spot and dare to fulfill your significance.

Elisha understood the law of honor. The law of honor states that what you honor will honor you. Essentially, the law of honor states that what you esteem will be exalted in your life. Your reward in life is the product of what you respect. Elijah told Elisha that he asked a hard thing. Nevertheless, if he saw him when he was taken it would be his. It was a hard thing but more importantly it was a heart thing. The heart is not just the organ that pumps the blood. It is the place of intentions. I refer to the heart as the epicenter of your life. Honor can never be displayed outwardly until it is first discerned inwardly. What am I saying? Your heart is the place of honor. The breakdown that I see in leadership around the world is a matter of the heart. It is not that we do not have smart and capable leaders. No, the problem is that we do not have sincere and compassionate leaders. You cannot lead from your head. When you lead from your head, systems collapse, institutions become broken and society becomes paralyzed. In contrast, when you lead from your heart systems are strengthened, institutions are anchored and society is empowered for progress. Elijah was saying to Elisha that if you honor me then you can have the mantle. Moreover, Elijah was saying your next season is being shaped by how you see me. The reason our world is broken is because we have leaders trying to lead from a place of blindness. When the blind lead the blind they all fall into a ditch. The ditch is simply a metaphor for an unproductive life characterized by uselessness. The school of the prophets already proved that they only saw Elijah as a teacher. They only followed for learning but they were never able to follow for legacy. Elisha is getting ready to prove that he saw Elijah as his future. It is impossible to say that you honor someone and your heart does not show it. I see it in families, organizations, governments and nations. We have people that tolerate each other but they have no honor for one another. I know that they do not honor one another because their hearts are filled with hatred and distrust. Disrespect is one of the greatest signs of dishonor. How you see the relationships in your life will demonstrate the level of honor those relationships hold in your life. You will always rebel against what you do not respect. We have produced a rebellious culture with no respect for leadership or authority. While I believe in being equitable in all relationships, I do not believe that equity is a concept that can define realms of power. I believe that every person is powerful and can reach their highest potential. Nonetheless, I also know that power and influence is distributed based on competency and capacity. In other words, we cannot all be equal in power because we are not all equal in position. This philosophy of equitable leadership is erroneous. At the end of the day, you are not on the same level with those that are your superiors. You can never make equal what has been elevated to a superior position of authority. Many people try to incorporate this principle of equity in leadership because they are rebellious and have no respect for leadership. Never forget that what you become familiar with ultimately becomes displaced and dishonored in your life. You cannot make common that which is uncommon. We are living in a generation that has lost respect and reverence for the rare.

How do you see the mentors and leaders in your life? Do you see them as friends, buddies or dumping grounds? Or do you see them as valuable, significant and wells of wisdom that have the power to shape your future? How you see your mentors and leaders will define the platforms that you stand on and the impact that you will have in the world. Familiarity is one of the greatest enemies of your future. I encourage you to guard against becoming familiar with your leaders and never see them as common. When you view your mentors and leaders as common, you constrict your progress and cripple your potential. Elisha never made the mistake of seeing Elijah as common. Elisha saw him as an important voice and significant teacher in his life. How Elisha saw Elijah shaped how he served him. Never once do we hear Elisha complaining about serving the senior prophet.

We see Elisha serving with joy and respect. His ability to perceive correctly is what positioned him to be able to ask such a bold question. Today, we have people trying to ask bold questions that have not qualified to access new realms. Honor is the result of being willing to sow your life into the vision of another man. Far too many people in the world today want to be master leaders when they have not first mastered following.

Why is submission and serving so important? Honor is something that has to be bestowed upon you. It is impossible and illegal to place honor on yourself. Honor comes from those that have witnessed and observed your life. Honor comes from those that can attest to your character, values, principles, temperament and attitude. Honor has to come from those that have seen you up close and can attest to your authenticity, accountability and track record. Honor comes from those that have seen you get into the trenches and facilitate the vision of another man. Honor has to come from those that can authenticate your journey from infancy to maturity. We have too many lone rangers in the world today that have never submitted or served anyone. As a result, these are the individuals that are rude, boastful and dictatorial in their leadership styles. The dishonorable always demand what they have never had the ability to demonstrate. Where can you lead people when you have never learned to follow? What insight can you offer your followers when you have never served the vision of another person? Do you even possess the equipment to empower and elevate other leaders? I've discovered in my journey that self sanctioned leaders are often self serving leaders. In other words, these are the kinds of leaders that never care about the growth, development and longevity of those that they lead. Leadership is simply a title if there is no leader to trace your mantle to. You can call yourself but you cannot choose yourself. Unfortunately, I have witnessed leaders that chose themselves and the aftermath was disastrous and destructive. Elisha qualified by exemplifying a life of service and submission. Your inability to see the value of leaders in your life will define your inability to lead anything meaningful and significant in the world. Anything great is built brick by brick. I believe this is a great analogy for leadership as well. No building has ever built itself. The most beautiful edifices and cathedrals in the world were built by master builders. Mentors, advisors and spiritual leaders in your life are master builders ensuring that your foundation is strong and your structure is solid. All great buildings have to be inspected and they must pass inspection before they can ever be occupied. All authentic leaders understand that no position of power can be occupied without proper inspection. Inspection is the only valid way to know that the building is built to last. However, if you manipulate the inspection then the integrity of the structure is compromised. When the structure of a building is compromised that building becomes condemned. What am I trying to say? Authentic power is the result of process and enduring leadership can only be occupied by that which has been proven. Honor is not proven by how we look but ultimately by how we live our lives. You must live your life in an honorable way.

In this moment of profound shifts and radical change in the world, I believe it is more important now than ever that we marry generations and master this law of honor. We have to reach across the aisle and be willing to disagree without being divided, have intense conversations without destroying relationships, and respect different viewpoints without silencing those voices in our lives. As you heard me state before, I have often had to sit at tables where I was the youngest and it was very uncomfortable. I have experienced lots of pushback and judgements from those that were older than me and did not respect or value my perspectives. However, I chose to not run away from the challenge but to embrace the challenge. I made the decision to stay seated at the table. First of all, I had every right to be at the table. Secondly, I understand that often we are waiting on things to change when God wants to make us the change. Lastly, I knew that without tension transformation would never happen. So I continued to sit at the table, share my perspectives, listen for insights and develop strategies to unite us all together around a common vision and mission. As a result, I learned a lot from senior leaders and they also learned from me. More importantly, a culture of respect and honor was created and the goals and objectives of various organizations were advanced. Many of you reading this book know exactly what I am talking about. You have said it would be easier for you to just leave and go somewhere else. While that would be the easy thing to do, that is not the most effective thing to do. If you want to be a great leader, then you have to learn how to handle conflict and understand that a difference of opinion does not have to divide an entire organization. Learn how to respect one another and see each person as a valuable contributor to the vision. I have seen the power of marrying generations through honor and it will be essential for organizations to thrive and prosper in the twenty-first century. You must understand that diverse perspectives propel organizations forward. Your ability to leverage difference will multiply your human capital and increase your economic capital astronomically. Difference is not an enemy to your organization. Difference is an engine that empowers the success and prosperity of your organization.

In closing, I want you to make a non-negotiable decision that you are going to put the law of honor into practice immediately. I want you to think of the relationships in your life that have become strained and fractured. Now think about how you can begin the process of refining and renegotiating the terms of the relationships in your life. You will never progress without honor. You will never grow or develop without honor. More importantly, you will never reach your greatest potential without honor. The reality is that we are all better together. One is not a powerful enough number to achieve greatness. Everything in this universe revolves around relationships. If you want to see rich and fulfilling relationships in your life then you need to master the law of honor. Realize that what you honor will honor you. On the other hand, what you dishonor will dishonor you. Your life is a reflection of what you respect. You are repelling everything that you do not respect. Respect defines the realm that you live from.

Honorable Living Exercises

1. Are you willing to do the work to help marry generations through honor?

2. Can you honestly say that you respect and honor the relationships in your life?

3. Is your life a reflection of a leader in authority and under authority?

4. What is your viewpoint on submission and accountability in leadership?

5. Do you have mentors in your life to equip, train and develop you?

6. Who do you honor?

7. How will you implement the law of honor in your life and leadership?

CHAPTER 10: THE DOUBLE PORTION

"Your posture and perception has everything to do with the portion you receive."

-Jamelle Sanders

And it came to pass, when they were gone over, that Elijah said unto Elisha, Ask what I shall do for thee, before I be taken away from thee. And Elisha said, I pray thee, let a double portion of thy spirit be upon me.

And he said, Thou hast asked a hard thing: nevertheless, if thou see me when I am taken from thee, it shall be so unto thee; but if not, it shall not be so.

And it came to pass, as they still went on, and talked, that, behold, there appeared a chariot of fire, and horses of fire, and parted them both asunder; and Elijah went up by a whirlwind into heaven.

And Elisha saw it, and he cried, My father, my father, the chariot of Israel, and the horsemen thereof. And he saw him no more: and he took hold of his own clothes, and rent them in two pieces.

He took up also the mantle of Elijah that fell from him, and went back, and stood by the bank of Jordan;

And he took the mantle of Elijah that fell from him, and smote the waters, and said, Where is the LORD God of Elijah? and when he also had smitten the waters, they parted hither and thither: and Elisha went over.

2nd Kings 2:9-14

While everything I have shared with you up until this point has been important, I believe that the principle that I am about to share with you is essential to the preservation of leadership for generations to come. If you recall, we just addressed the law of honor in the previous chapter. I tried to make it clear that the only way that you can marry generations is through honor. More importantly, I provided strategy and insights into how to do this effectively and what the results will be. If you will put this law of honor into practice, it will revolutionize your life, finances, relationships, your career and even cities and nations. The greatest human problems can all be traced back to a lack of honor. As long as we do not honor one another as human beings, we will continue to perpetuate vicious cycles of hatred, bigotry, apathy and injustice. However, when we honor one another we heal ourselves and we heal the world. This is truly the heart of my life and work. I want people around the world to awaken to their significance so we can ultimately awaken society and alter systems and institutions forever. Honor is a powerful law and force that we have not even begun to utilize effectively. So make the decision to live a life of honor. It begins with honoring yourself and then you can honor the other relationships in your life. Honor begins with our ability to celebrate our differences and make a decision to listen and understand.

This powerful text of Elijah and Elisha is one of my personal favorites. I cannot tell you how many times I have read it. Furthermore, I cannot begin to explain all the principles and insights I have gained from this text. Several years ago I gave a keynote on mantles. It was a powerful teaching that still resonates with me even until this day. I believe that you were made to live a meaningful life. In addition, I believe that you have been mantled for a mandate in your lifetime and generation. Notice that I just said that you have been mantled for a mandate. A mantle gives you power and authority to operate in a sphere of influence and to dominate a measure of rule. For the sake of time, I will not go into great detail about the definition and meaning of mantles because it would take me too much time. However, I will say that every person on this planet has been mantled to do something. In fact, I will share that in my years of study and research I have discovered that mantles can fall into over thirty different categories. Many people just peruse the bible but they fail to perceive that the bible is replete with examples of individuals that found their mantles and fulfilled their missions in the world. Many people would say that Elisha was meant to be an entrepreneur and run the family empire. However, I will venture out to say that Elisha was mantled to be a prophetic voice to the nations. If Elisha would have never left the comforts of home, he would have never collided with heaven's original plan and purpose for his life. Many of you reading this book are getting ready to have an awakening. You are going to come to the realization that you were made for more and that there is something that you have been mantled to do in your lifetime and generation. God never gives you an assignment without empowering you with a mantle to accomplish that assignment. In this keynote that I delivered years ago, I talked about the importance of not forfeiting the mantle. It is very important that you understand the power of perception. Elijah said to Elisha that he asked a very hard thing. Nevertheless, if Elisha saw Elijah when he was taken then the mantle was his. I want to address a very important principle. It is very possible to be in the presence of greatness and yet not perceive greatness. Why do I say this? The school of the prophets were present when Elijah went up in the whirlwind. Therefore, we can conclude that attendance is not a qualifier for a mantle. Elijah was not just talking about being present when he was taken. Elijah was saying that you have to be perceptive when I am taken. Perception has to do with much more than your sight. Perception has to deal with spiritual acumen and perceptivity. In other words, if you have the ability to perceive what has been destined for you then you can possess the double portion. Notice I did not say that you can have the mantle because you have potential or an inkling of your destiny. Inklings and impressions do not give you insight into prophetic realms. You will never unlock a realm without recognition. Recognition is always the womb of release.

One of the most important truths that you can ever discover is that in order to access a mantle it often comes through mentorship. More importantly, in order to access the mantle of Elijah it was vital that Elisha was clear about what Elijah meant to him and the weight he held in his life. Elijah makes a profound statement that if you see me when I am taken then the mantle will transfer to you. Didn't everyone see Elijah? What exactly did the senior prophet mean by seeing him? Elijah was not talking about observation but identification. In other words, if you will identify my role in your life then heaven will release the mantle to you. For a moment, I thought that Elisha was going to forfeit the mantle. It seemed that as Elijah was going up in the whirlwind that nothing was happening. I was saying internally that this cannot be how this is going to end. This man has served faithfully for years and left everything to follow Elijah. Surely, the story is not going to end with his mentor being taken and the mantle not being transferred to Elisha. However, as I excavated the text I finally got the revelation. If Elisha could see Elijah as more than a teacher, mentor or prophet then he would access the mantle. The question was not whether or not Elisha qualified for the mantle. The question was would Elisha ask the right question to access the mantle. In other words, how Elisha saw Elijah was the key to unlocking the next season of his life. The school of the prophets acknowledged Elijah as a great teacher and prophet. However, that was the extent of the relationship. On the other hand, Elisha saw Elijah as his destiny. Elisha saw Elijah as his father. The moment he saw Elijah as his father the mantle fell. In essence, identity always determines inheritance. The double portion is always reserved for those that are in your prophetic posterity. As Elisha identified Elijah as his father, we see the transfer of mantles and anointings to the next generation.

As a prophetic voice to my generation, God has given me a tremendous responsibility to mentor, advise and develop many leaders for the Kingdom of God. It is a responsibility that I take very seriously because I know that God will hold me accountable. Also, I want to say that I do not just mentor and develop anybody. Only after prayerful consideration and a divine prompting from God do I begin any mentoring relationship. What I have discovered about mentorship is that when it comes to your professional development you often have the pleasure of choosing your mentors. However, when it comes to your spiritual growth and development, you do not always have a choice in who your mentor will be. We often gravitate towards those that we have an affinity for. However, God often assigns us to those that will adjust us so we can embrace the fullness of our assignments. Also, another reason we do not often get to choose our spiritual mentors is because we are looking through our natural eyes. We often lack the discernment and proficiency to perceive those that have the spiritual tools and keys to unlock the treasures that God has placed inside of us. Rarely are we drawn to those that carry the DNA of our destinies. Mentorship is not about inspiration but imparation. Mentors hold master keys that shape our character, build our capacity and unlock the greatness on the inside of us. Your inability to discern those that God has assigned to help you fulfill your destiny will create cycles of frustration, failure and defeat in your life. You will never triumph until you find your tribe. Your tribe is essential to your training, transformation and triumph.

We all know that every child gets their DNA from their father. With that said, I will venture out to say that you can trace the authenticity of any anointing or mantle back to a legitimate apostolic or prophetic father. As I look around the world today, I see a tremendous leadership challenge in this generation. I have had the privilege of mentoring many over the years. What I have discovered is that there is a lack of authentic mantles and anointings because many have lacked true fathers. Unfortunately, we have many that have called themselves but they were never chosen by God. I can study their spiritual DNA and trace their spiritual lineage to uncredible leadership and illegitimate authority. According To 1st Corinthians 4:15, "For though ye have ten thousand instructors in Christ, yet have ye not many fathers: for in Christ Jesus I have begotten you through the gospel." I am sure some of you have read or even preached this particular verse. However, not many have cracked the prophetic code that is hidden in this verse of scripture. I have seen many instructors in the body of Christ. On the other hand, I have seen a scarcity of true fathers. The role of a father is not to soothe and comfort you. No, the role of a father is to train, develop, discipline and birth you out in the spirit. I believe that over the years we have had many that meant well but they were never mantled to take on the role and responsibility of spiritual fathers. As a result, they sent sons out undeveloped and unequipped for the challenges that come with fulfilling prophetic destiny. When it comes to being birthed out for Kingdom impact, you do not just need a pastor but a spiritual father. Pastors have a heart to protect the sheep from harm or danger. Conversely, fathers have the important responsibility of molding, shaping, maturing, developing and growing spiritually mature sons and daughters. Fathers are stern because they realize that they have the enormous responsibility of stretching you and helping to steward the gifts that God has given you. A pastor will be content with your membership. On the contrary, fathers are consumed with your maturation and mastery. While many of these spiritual leaders had good intentions, they lacked the equipment to effectively empower these sons and daughters to step into their destinies. The danger in this is that it can cause a person to mount platforms that they have not been matured and processed to stand on. It is one thing to see the gifts within a person. It is another thing to know how to cultivate those gifts and develop the character of that individual for greatness. Fathers both sharpen and shape us so that we are empowered to fulfill prophetic destiny. In fact, I will venture out to say that you will never fulfill your prophetic destiny without a father. Fathers possess both the experience and equipment needed to sharpen you and shift you into prophetic destiny.

Why has it been a lack of authentic spiritual fathers? One thing I always tell people in mentorship is that you should never take advice from individuals that have not been where you are trying to go. The problem is that we have many offering advice but lacking experience. A spiritual father is a guide that gives you the opportunity to extract wisdom from their journey and experiences. We have too many people that have never been birthed out trying to birth out leaders. They are illegitimate and they are detrimental to the progress of the Kingdom of God. The reason we have seen a lack of spiritual fathers is because not everyone has the capacity to pull out of you what God has put in you. Fathers not only speak to your potential but they have the prophetic license and apostolic authority to draw out of you what was divinely downloaded in your DNA before the foundation of the world. You need to stop being enamored by people that can see your potential. Start embracing the individuals that can empower you to maximize your greatest potential. It is nothing more frustrating than to be pregnant with something that nobody around you can perceive or help to push out. Spiritual fathers are essential because they have the skill, wisdom, insight and capacity to help you give birth to your prophetic destiny. Only a spiritual father has the ability to speak to who you were destined to be and help shape you to fulfill that destiny. You do not need cheerleaders. You need a father that can build your capacity for greatness and success. You need to be birthed out to become who you were born to be!

We can now conclude that the mantle did not fall until Elisha identified Elijah as his father. From in depth research, I can make the observation that double portions belong to sons. More importantly, double portions belong to the eldest son. The double portion was the father's way of ensuring that the inheritance went to the son and that no illegitimate party had a right to lay claim to what was rightfully his. While Elijah had no natural children, Elijah had a spiritual son named Elisha. We know that Elisha served faithfully for many years without title, recognition or fanfare. Elisha recklessly abandoned everything to follow this prophet with no guarantee of success. All Elisha had was a word from God and prophetic insight to see a reality not yet born to time. Elisha understood that service was a prophetic catalyst to the double portion. Furthermore, Elisha realized that it was not enough to respect what was on the life of Elijah. Elisha understood that recognition is the key to unlocking realms of favor and Kingdom greatness. In fact, recognition is the key to receiving anything in the Kingdom of God. As we see this powerful prophetic picture playing out, we see Elijah going up into heaven by a whirlwind. Elisha was in a state of grief as his spiritual father is transitioning into eternity. However, I am sure that Elisha is still perplexed by what Elijah meant when he said you must see me when I am taken to get the double portion. Now we see Elijah going up and Elisha finally has a revelation. Elisha recognizes that Elijah was not just a mentor, advisor or spiritual teacher. No, Elisha realizes that Elijah is his father. Elisha then calls Elijah father and the mantle begins to fall. Elisha recognized in that moment why he had to leave the oxen and give up the family business. Elisha recognized why he had been serving faithfully and pouring water on the hands of Elijah for all these years. Elisha recognized why he had to pass all the tests for promotion. It becomes crystal clear to Elisha that he has been in the middle of a prophetic process. All these experiences have been divinely engineered to bring him into his prophetic destiny. I want you to understand that Elijah was not talking about seeing him with the natural eye. Elijah was talking about seeing him through the eye of honor. In other words, Elijah was saying if you master the law of honor you can have the double portion. Many people run up in prayer lines to receive double portions. While this is admirable, I want you to understand that you are not entitled to receive any anointing that you have not served. It would be illegal and a violation of the laws of the Kingdom. Elisha received the double portion because he sowed his entire life in service to God and Elijah. What have you given up? Never think that little sacrifice will produce great rewards. No mantle is given without a heavy price. God only places weight on the trustworthy. You cannot be found trustworthy until you have been through the fire. If you want to shoulder great glory, then I want you to know that you must be willing to sacrifice greatly.

This is a perfect picture of succession in leadership. Elijah and Elisha show us how to transfer power from one generation to another. The great travesty of the twenty-first century is that we have success without successors. I have watched great leaders go on and observed as ministries, organizations, systems and institutions collapsed. Why did this happen? The leader did a great job of building the vision but a horrible job at building the people. What good does it do to build great buildings only to have them torn down after you die? No vision can long endure without great people. The development of people is one of the only ways you can create a lasting legacy. Otherwise, we live forgettable lives that have no impact on future generations. It should be the goal of every great leader to create something that outlives you. It is important that you take the time to not only grow yourself but to grow the people around you. Elijah poured tirelessly into Elisha for years. At the same time. Elisha honored the wisdom of Elijah and used it to grow, develop and manifest Kingdom greatness. Never waste energy pouring into empty places. Pour into the teachable, hungry and those that passionately pursue. I know from experience that pursuit determines your portion. I see so many people in the world with great potential and good intentions. However, they are lacking in the area of pursuit. Pursuit is the womb of possibilities. Pursuit is the catalyst to promotion. Pursuit is the doorway into prophetic destiny. Ultimately, pursuit determines your progress and prosperity. If you want to fulfill purpose and maximize your greatest potential then you must become a person of pursuit. You have to pursue in the good times, bad times, hard times, trying times, frustrating times and even pressure times. You cannot allow difficulties and challenges to define your pursuit. While Elisha served faithfully for years, I am sure that he had moments of frustration, fatigue and even discouragement. Elisha understood that he could not allow anything to deter him from his destiny. No matter how uncomfortable or uncertain things became he was unshakeable in his commitment to his spiritual father and the fulfillment of his prophetic destiny.

In order to access the double portion, you must understand that you cannot have the double portion without being proven. Pursuit always proves what the most important priorities are in your life. I cannot tell you how many people have come to me for mentorship and advising. Then a couple of months go by and I never hear from them again. What happened? Most people are not willing to pursue it. Furthermore, most people are not willing to go through the prophetic process and be developed. Mentorship is something that has to be pursued. I will never chase a person that considers me a mentor. If what I carry is valuable enough for you to consider me a mentor, then you must be willing to commit to pursuing what is on my life. I will make myself available. However, when I do not see pursuit I revoke access to me because a person has shown that they do not value me or what I possess. How are you proven? You are only proven when pressure is applied. The reason many people come to me for mentorship and never return is because they cannot handle the proving season. Most people give up in times of pressure. I have learned to see pressure as a gift in my life. Pressure has refined my character, tested my commitments, defined my priorities, built my capacity and taught me invaluable lessons. When a mentor applies pressure to the life of a mentee, this is when the authenticity of that relationship is proven. Unfortunately, what I have observed is that people will admire what you carry but very few are willing to be adjusted to unleash their own capacity for greatness. Mentors do not show up in your life to caress and console you. No, mentors show up in your life to correct and calibrate you. You cannot reach your highest altitude in life without adjustment. Adjustment ensures the authenticity of your leadership and influence. The preservation of your leadership demands that you are proven. Only after you are proven can you become powerful.

Elisha reached that same tipping point in his relationship with Elijah. We see in the text how Elijah tried to shake him and how his commitment was tested. I want to stop and say that crises and challenges will always test your commitment. You are not tested in the easy things. You are tested in the challenging times. You are tested when you find yourself internally conflicted between the easy thing and the ethical thing. You are tested when you are torn between good over great, morality over immorality, integrity over compromise, politics over principles and truth over deception. It is only when pressure is applied to our lives that we truly become acquainted with who we are and what we possess. We see in that moment that Elisha chose destiny over distractions. Elisha had paid a heavy price and he was determined to go all the way. I have seen many people start out with good intentions in leadership. However, they did not have the stamina and the standards to go all the way. Elisha realized that all progress is painful. In essence, anything you gain in life will be the product of growth. We do not grow in pristine places. We grow under pressure. Pressure is the catalyst for promotion. Pressure is what will usher you into prophetic destiny. So many people want great responsibility but they are unwilling to pay a great price. The double portion is going to cost you. What is it going to cost you? Convenience, comfort, time, energy, resources, relationships and even preconceived notions and ideas. The double portion will require that you give up everything that you think you know to pursue a reality that is unborn to time. The double portion will require you to lose yourself in order to find your true identity and fulfill your Kingdom assignment. The double portion will require you to live like no one else so you can live like no one else. What Elisha gave up could not compare to what God entrusted him with. Every sacrifice Elisha made was the seed for future seasons of significance in his life. We talk about double portions but very few people are willing to pay the price for the double portion. Are you willing to be inconvenienced to give birth to infinite possibilities for your life? Can you endure hardship to produce future seasons of honor in your life? Will you dare to allow difficulties to produce diamonds in your life? The double portion belongs to the person that is willing to abandon everything in order to fulfill the assignment of eternity. The double portion is the product of sacrificing today in order to embrace the significance of tomorrow. The double portion belongs to the one that will dare to use the currency of faith to seed the future and birth a reality not yet known to time.

How can Elijah give Elisha double when he does not have double? This is a question that I want you to ponder for a moment. Elijah had no double portion to give Elisha. However, his seasons of sacrifice, seed of service and ability to see Elijah as his prophetic father opened the portals of heaven. Not only that, but Elisha literally pulled a double portion out of eternity and into time. Elisha's faith and faithfulness gave creative force to the womb of the spirit causing heaven to contract and release what he asked for. How could Elisha ask for this? Elisha could ask for a double portion because he was aligned with his father. As a result of Elijah and Elisha having the same heart alignment, heaven honored Elisha's request. A lot of people are asking for double portions but they never acquired the father's heart. Without the father's heart, you will always be asking but never acquiring because you still have your own agenda. Heaven will consider your request illegitimate until God can recognize the identity of your father in you.

Elisha was able to boldly ask for the double portion because he possessed the DNA of Elijah. What we need in this era is less talking and more leaders whose anointings and mantles can be traced back to legitimate apostolic and prophetic fathers. What we need is a generation that will humble themselves before God so heaven can honor them. What we need are people with no egos that simply want to see the agenda of eternity fulfilled. We are on the prophetic and apostolic precipice of the greatest release of mantles and anointings the world has ever seen. The hearts of the children are being turned back to the fathers. In addition, the hearts of the fathers are being turned back to the children. As a result, we are getting ready to see a marrying of mantles and anointings. When the fathers and the sons become one, we will see great outpourings, great reformation and great advancement of the Kingdom of God. When we see the fathers and sons become one, we will see the greatest expression of God that the world has ever known. The father and son relationship is the greatest expression of the Kingdom of God in the earth realm. Systems will be revolutionized, institutions will be rebuilt and kingdoms will be brought under the rulership of Christ once and for all. The manifestation of the Sons of God is the manifestation of the Kingdom. I have served faithfully in ministry serving my leaders and I will continue to serve them. I have had to be rebuked, corrected, adjusted and challenged many times. However, I am so grateful for it all today. It did not feel good at the time but it forged in me something that has made me unbreakable and unstoppable. People admire the anointing on my life and the influence that God has given me. I want you to know that I would not be who I am without great spiritual leadership and accountability in my life. I do not mind taking out the trash, scrubbing toilets, vacuuming floors or even washing the dishes. Why? I understand that double portions belong to sons and sons are servants. The greatest in the Kingdom is a servant. Elsiah understood this and that is why he walked in the double portion anointing. Never reach for a mantle until you have first married the heart of your spiritual father. In a generation of gifted people, I say to you that you need spiritual fathers and mothers to mold you so that when your moment comes you will not forfeit the mantle. Pursue the double portion!

Honorable Living Exercises

1. Have you made the decision to first honor yourself so you can honor the other relationships in your life?

2. What have you been mantled to do in your generation?

3. Who are the mentors in your life?

4. When we look at your spiritual DNA, can we trace it back to a spiritual father?

5. Who have you served selflessly and sacrificially?

6. Have you been proven in order to be entrusted with power?

Afterword

Honestly, as I wrote the last chapter of this book the anointing came upon me so strongly that I could hardly contain myself. I believe that what you have just read are key apostolic and prophetic strategies for the next generation of leaders. For too long we have seen success without successors. This book is pregnant with wisdom, insights and strategies for successfully transferring power from one generation to the next. My prayer is that this will be so much more than a book. It is my prayer and intention that this will incite a revolution of leadership. May you be compelled to take action and make a difference in your lifetime and generation. I know that it will take you some time to digest all of the principles that I have shared with you in this book. However, if you will just take action on one of these principles every day it will radically change your life. I wrote this book because I wanted to create a tool for leaders that are in the process of mentoring and developing leaders and those that are transitioning and thinking about their successors. The days of simply filling positions with individuals that lack the capacity to bring solutions and change are over. We need leaders that can occupy positions and possess the capacity, intellectual prowess and solutions to make an impact where they are assigned. That is why I wrote this book and it is my prayer that this is the reason that you picked up this book in the first place. *Honor* is about restoring authenticity and integrity to the position of leadership

    Honor is more than a message to me. This is a principle that I live by and a law that I impart into those that I have been assigned to mentor and develop for leadership. While I believe it is important for leaders to have a vast repository of wisdom and experiences, I believe that it is even more important that leaders possess honor. If you want to influence people and have others follow you, then you have to live an honorable life. Unfortunately, what I have seen over the years is individuals demanding honor from others without demonstrating an honorable life. I strive with everything in me to live an honorable life. I believe it is the reason that my life and work has resonated with people in such a profound way. In addition, I believe that is one of the primary reasons I have been able to establish an unprecedented connection with people all over the world. I believe that leadership is a privilege and influence is sacred. What do I mean by that? When I say that influence is sacred I mean that it is something that should never be abused or misused. Power that is not governed by convictions will corrupt a person. I have seen it happen so many times. That is why it is so important that you consistently check your motives for leadership. I am honored to have received numerous awards and accolades. However, I remain centered on my intention to use my power and influence to make a difference in the world. I realize that my platform is so much bigger than me. My platform gives me the opportunity to amplify the voices of others and to be a voice for the voiceless. Never try to express a message until you have first embodied the message. As I always tell my mentees, people are not just listening to your words but they are looking at the way you live your life. This is why we cannot theorize leadership. No, leadership must become a way of being.

In the days to come, I hope that you will refer to this resource over and over again. I hope it finds its way into schools, universities, businesses, cities, communities, nations and ultimately the entire world. I believe that if we all live by the principles in this book we can truly make this world a better place. If you have followed my work over the years, you know that I am highly respected as a thought leader and leadership specialist. People from around the world reach out to me for leadership training, leadership development and leadership consulting. Leadership is one of my greatest passions because I know that it holds the key to creating an empowered world. At the time that I am writing this to you, the world is dealing with a global pandemic and a racial uprising that is creating unrest and revealing the brokenness of systems and institutions. Now more than ever before people are reaching out to me for solutions and strategies for leading in moments of crisis. I am so glad that this book is being released now. This book is both timely and prophetic for the days that we are living in. Clearly, we need honorable leaders now more than ever to rise to the highest heights of leadership in this nation. We need leaders with convictions and compassion to speak truth to power and to bring transformation to systems, institutions and communities. Make the decision that you are going to be part of this new generation of emerging leaders and take your place. The world needs you now more than ever!

Honor is a book that will speak to you for generations to come. This is truly a labor of love for me. I have spoken and delivered key notes on this principle of honor. However, I felt like I had so much more to say so I decided to put those ideas in a book. As I developed my ideas, it started to pour out of me like a well. I knew that the concepts and strategies in this book would be revolutionary and challenge the world to lead at a different level. You all know me well enough that I do not write just for the sake of writing. I write to empower, provoke thought, compel action and incite change in the hearts of people all around the world. That is exactly what I am praying that this book will do. I see every single day the need for leadership. I have written about this for so many years and I have devoted my life to developing leaders that will make a difference in the world. It is time for you to shift your consciousness, awaken to your power and occupy your position of influence. This is not the time for passivity and complacency.

This is a time for action and progress. The world needs servant leadership. You have been called to lead in your generation. There is something that you have been mantled to do. Whether you lead in industry, politics, science, education, technology, media or even sports, every leader is important and you must use your voice to bring change to the world and its communities. I have never been more excited. While many people are discouraged and disillusioned, I am energized and empowered. As I speak with leaders in finance, business, education, government, technology and many other spheres I see this as a moment of major shifts and profound change in the world. I believe in you and I believe in the greatness that lives on the inside of you. It is time for you to dare to lead with honor and integrity and to manifest your greatness. It is impossible to truly live a meaningful life if your life does not multiply. Leadership gives us the incredible opportunity to multiply our lives and to impact generations to come. Honor will not only promote you but preserve the integrity of what you build for successive generations.

Declarations of Honor

- I decree that I make a vowel and personal commitment to live a life of honor.
- I decree that I will be honorable in my thoughts, words and actions.
- I decree that honor will promote me to the highest positions of leadership and influence in the world.
- I decree that my character is being refined, my attitude adjusted and my life calibrated to step into the magnitude of what I was created for.
- I decree that I possess the competency, capacity, character and courage to lead with morality, dignity and hope.
- I decree that I will never compromise my principles and convictions.
- I decree that I give myself the gift of goodbye and say goodbye to a horrible past in order to embrace an extraordinary future.

- I decree that I recklessly abandon everything that restricts my ascension into realms of power, influence, affluence, wealth and success.
- I decree that I renegotiate the terms of every relationship in my life.
- I decree that I will no longer settle for second-class, dysfunctional, destiny-abortive relationships in my life.
- I decree that I embrace divinely ordained relationships.
- I decree that I possess prophetic acumen and perceptivity.
- I decree that with laser sharp discernment and clear vision I discern my tribe and those that you have assigned to be part of my destiny.
- I decree that I will squeeze the value, wisdom and lessons out of every season.
- I decree that I am maturing and know when to say goodbye to an old season and hello to exciting new chapters in my life.

- I decree that I am willing to leave the security of today in order to embrace the significance of tomorrow.
- I decree that my heritage, community, family and history will not define my destiny.
- I decree that when the invitation for greatness is extended to me that I will accept the invitation and decline anything that perpetuates mediocrity, ordinary and second-class living.
- I decree that I will pursue mentorship, live responsibly and seek out accountability as a leader.
- I decree that I am submitted to spiritual leadership and I am not a lone ranger.
- I decree that I have strong spiritual leaders in my life to challenge me, correct me, calibrate me and build the capacity in me to fulfill my purpose and maximize my greatest potential.
- I decree that I do not become offended with spiritual leaders when they challenge my excuses, identity flaws in

my character and demand my growth and maturity.

- I decree that I make a conscious decision to grow, develop and mature on a daily basis.
- I decree that I am willing to sow my life into the vision of those that I have been assigned to serve.
- I decree that when I am tested in my commitment to my spiritual leaders I will pass the test.
- I decree that I will pay the price for the double portion.
- I decree that I will honor and respect the spiritual leaders and mentors that I have been assigned to.
- I decree that I will complete every assignment with excellence and always be exceptional in everything that I do.
- I decree I embrace correction and use it as a prophetic tool to sharpen my edge.
- I decree that I will remain teachable and pliable.
- I decree that I will not bring reproach or shame to leadership.

- I decree that integrity and authenticity are pillars in my life.
- I decree that I am not one that fills a position of leadership. Instead, I am mantled to occupy positions of leadership.
- I decree that I will have success with successors.
- I decree that I will work to marry generations through honor.

Declarations of Honor

- I decree that my life is governed by the law of honor.
- I decree that I am honored by all who know me, meet me, or have any kind of formal or informal dealings with me.
- I decree that I live a respectable life and that I have a reputation of honor and integrity.
- I decree that I seek out counsel and wisdom from the spiritual leaders in my life.
- I decree that I will never waste the time of my spiritual leaders. I will always value their time and cherish the moments that I spend with them.
- I decree that I will always honor leaders in their presence and in their absence.
- I decree that I will listen, learn and apply the wisdom that my spiritual leaders share with me.
- I decree that I will not make the job of my spiritual leaders grievous by refusing to grow and develop.

- I decree that my spiritual leaders can depend on me to help shoulder the responsibilities of leadership.
- I decree that I am proven and as a result I am entrusted with great power and responsibilities.
- I decree that I will not forfeit my mantle.
- I decree that I will master the sphere of influence that God has assigned me to.
- I decree that I will be positioned, perceive and seize key moments of opportunity.
- I decree that I will master the law of asking and use it as a prophetic tool to unlock seasons of answers, awakening and acceleration in my life.
- I decree that I will never again curse my destiny but I will reframe the questions that I am asking.
- I decree that I will cooperate with the prophetic process.
- I decree that I will allow pressure to prove me.
- I decree that I will learn to see pressure as a gift in my life.
- I decree that pressure will be the catalyst to my promotion and prosperity.

- I decree that I will commit to greatness.
- I decree that I will eliminate excuses and exemplify a life of excellence.
- I decree that I am living a world-class life.
- I decree that I will not play small but dare to play a bigger game.
- I decree that nothing will be able to divide me from my destiny.
- I decree that nothing will be able to move me off of my mission.
- I decree that when I am prompted from within I will listen for God's voice.
- I decree that when God directs me to move I will not hesitate.
- I decree that I will have the courage to follow the voice of God over my thoughts and emotions.
- I decree that I will not prolong seasons and perpetuate cycles in my life.
- I decree that when my future calls me I will have the audacity to answer it.
- I decree that I will dare to pursue the reality of God for my life that is not yet known to time.
- I decree that I am synchronized and syncopated with heaven's rhythm.

- I decree that I will have the faith to step out on a word from God even when I am not sure of my next steps.
- I decree that the pieces of my prophetic puzzle are coming together.
- I decree that obedience is bringing me into my ordained place.
- I decree that the currency of faith is carving a prophetic pathway into my future.
- I decree that as I remain aligned I arrive at my prophetic destiny on time and in season.
- I decree that I will serve my generation and transfer mantles.

ABOUT THE AUTHOR

Jamelle Sanders is a life and business strategist, author, speaker, mentor, highly respected thought leader and leading empowerment specialist. As one of the most respected voices in the world, he is committed to helping leaders and entrepreneurs succeed by sharing the secrets and systems that have contributed to his success. This commitment encompasses books, live events, training systems and programs. Jamelle is a regular contributor to The Huffington Post, Elite Daily, Thrive Global and numerous other media platforms. Jamelle has successfully empowered leaders and entrepreneurs around the world to succeed in life and business.